SADLIER PHONICS

Level C

Lesley Mandel Morrow
Senior Author

Marie Garman   **Patricia Maureen Mount**   **Patricia Scanlon**

Literacy Consultants

Heather K. Casey, Ph.D.
Department of Teacher Education
Rider University

Ernest Morrell, Ph.D.
Graduate School of Education
University of California, Los Angeles

Jennifer Rowsell, Ph.D.
Graduate School of Education
Rutgers University

Erica C. Boling, Ph.D.
Graduate School of Education
Rutgers University

Robert Calfee, Ph.D.
Graduate School of Education
University of California, Riverside

Robert Rueda, Ph.D.
Rossier School of Education
University of Southern California

Carmelita Williams, Ed.D.
Graduate School of Education
Norfolk State University

Cheryl Dyer
Assistant Superintendent
Bridgewater-Raritan (NJ) School District

Eleanor M. Vargas
Teacher Education Department
Claremont Graduate University

Diane H. Tracey, Ed.D.
College of Education
Kean University

D. Ray Reutzel, Ph.D.
Emma Eccles Jones College of Education
and Human Services
Utah State University

Printed in the United States of America   ISBN: 978-0-8215-7903-9   14 15 16 WEBC 20 19 18

Contents

★ **Essential Foundational Skill**

4 r-Controlled Vowels, Vowel Digraphs, and Diphthongs
Theme: Super Sports

5 Syllables, Contractions, and Word Endings
Theme: Genius at Work

★ **Essential Foundational Skill**

★ **Essential Foundational Skill**

Autumn Leaves

One of the nicest beds I know
isn't a bed of soft white snow,
isn't a bed of cool green grass
after the noisy mowers pass,
isn't a bed of yellow hay
making me itch for half a day—
but autumn leaves in a pile *that* high,
deep, and smelling like fall, and dry.
That's the bed where I like to lie
and watch the flutters of fall go by.

Aileen Fisher

Critical Thinking Would you prefer to lie on a bed of white snow, green grass, yellow hay, or autumn leaves? Explain your choice. Where would you go to watch "the flutters of fall" go by?

Name _____

Dear Family,

As your child progresses through this unit about autumn, she or he will review the sounds of the consonants. The 21 letters of the alphabet that are consonants are shown below.

- Say the name of each consonant.

Apreciada Familia,

Al tiempo que los niños progresan en esta unidad acerca del otoño, repasarán los sonidos de las consonantes. Las 21 letras consonantes del alfabeto se muestran más abajo.

- Pronuncien el nombre de cada consonante.

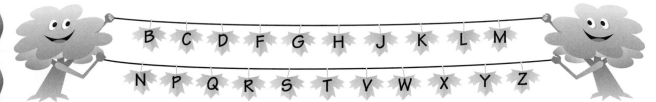

B C D F G H J K L M
N P Q R S T V W X Y Z

- Read the poem on the reverse side. Talk about the colors and smell of autumn leaves.

- Read the poem again, pausing after each pair of rhyming lines.

- See how many of the 21 consonants you and your child can find in the poem.

- Lean el poema en la página 5. Hablen sobre los colores y los olores de las hojas del otoño.

- Lean de nuevo el poema pausando después de cada par de versos.

- Miren cuantas consonantes pueden encontrar en el poema.

l leaves, listen
m maple, mowers
n nuts, nice
p pumpkin, party
q quiet
r rake, ripple
s spin
t tumble, tree

See the maple leaves spin in the air.

PROJECT

On a blank sheet of paper, help your child list the consonants from **b** to **z**. Next to each letter, have your child write one or two words that begin with the consonant sound. Together, use some of the words to write several sentences or a poem about autumn.

PROYECTO

En una hoja de papel en blanco hagan una lista de las consonantes de la **b** a la **z**. Al lado de cada letra escriban una o dos palabras que empiecen con el sonido de esa consonante. Use algunas de las palabras para escribir oraciones o un poema acerca del otoño.

Name _____

Here's a Hint! The letters **b, c, d, f, g, h, j, k, l, m, n, p, q, r, s, t, v, w, x, y,** and **z** are **consonants.**

Say the name of the picture. **Circle** the consonant that stands for the beginning sound.

1.	n z s	2.	r c v	3.	x l b
4.	k w h	5.	j y g	6.	d k f
7.	y z k	8.	m qu p	9.	v b w

Circle and **write** the word that completes each sentence.

10. This _____ day is cool and sunny.   fall   tall

11. So hurry up, lazybones! Get out of _____.   wed   bed

12. Put on a sweater and warm wool _____.   socks   locks

13. It's _____ to rake up the autumn leaves.   dime   time

14. Help me _____ a great big pile.   make   bake

15. On your mark, get set, _____!   lump   jump

Lesson 2 • Recognizing and Writing Initial Consonants   **7**

Consonants

Say the name of the picture. Write the consonant that stands for the ending sound.

1. [web] ☐	2. [bus] ☐	3. [coat] ☐
4. [bug] ☐	5. [broom] ☐	6. [wheel] ☐
7. [clap] ☐	8. [fox] ☐	9. [cloud] ☐

Make plans for the fall. Circle and write the word that completes each item on the list.

Autumn Plans

✓ _____ for flying ants.   Loop   Look

✓ Watch the _____ set early.   sub   sun

✓ See the harvest _____ rise.   moon   moose

✓ Make a _____ rubbing.   leap   leaf

✓ _____ some popcorn.   Pop   Pod

✓ Study _____ this year at school. hark hard

Write on Track

Add your own autumn plans to the list. Circle words that end in a single consonant sound.

PHONICS ALIVE AT HOME

Ask your child to say another word that ends with the same consonant sound as each picture name in items 1–9.

Name _____

Say the name of the picture. **Write** the consonant or consonants that stand for the middle sound.

1. ca___in	**2.** spi___er	**3.** mi___en
4. bo___es	**5.** ro___in	**6.** mo___ey
7. ba___oon	**8.** bea___er	**9.** Au___ust

Word Strategy You can use consonant sounds and context clues to help you read an unknown word.

Write a word from the box to complete each sentence. Use the word strategy to help you.

spider	August	beaver	autumn	robin

10. _____ is the last full month of summer.

11. In _____ we get ready for winter.

12. A _____ stores twigs and sticks at the bottom of a pond.

13. A _____ spins a strong web.

14. A _____ flies south for the winter.

Review

Say the name of the picture. **Write** the consonants that stand for the missing sounds.

1.  ___oa___	**2.**  ___e___o___	**3.**  ___oo___
4.  ___ea___u___	**5.**  ___ar___	**6.** ___a___o___
7. ___o___	**8.** ___a___a___	**9.** **7** ___e___e___

Use each pair of words to **write** a sentence about autumn.

10. yellow, leaf _____

_____

11. autumn, cool _____

_____

12. rake, pile _____

_____

13. wood, cabin _____

_____

PHONICS ALIVE AT HOME — Ask your child to write sentences about spring, using each pair of words: **rain, mud; red, tulip;** and **robin, bunny.**

Name _____

Here's a Hint! S can st nd for more than one sound.

sun   hose   ti**ss**ue

Say the name of the picture. **Circle** the words that have the same **s** sound as the picture name.

1. 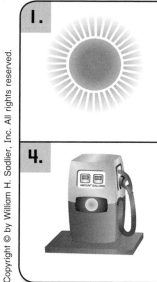	socce rose seven bus	**2.**  cheese his sun pies
		3. 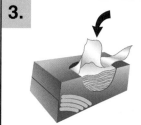 sugar same hose daisy

1. 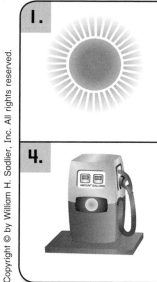 socce / rose / seven / bus

2.  cheese / his / sun / pies

3. 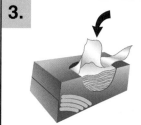 sugar / same / hose / daisy

4.  yes / soon / was / grass

5. soap / gas / tissue / sure

6. music / sand / busy / peas

Write the word from above that fits each clue.

7. This is a team sport play d in the fall.   _____

8. This is what you use to w ter the garden.   _____

9. This is how you feel when ou know the answer.   _____

10. This is the number of days n a week.   _____

11. This is the sound made wh n you sing.   _____

12. This is what you use when ou have a cold.   _____

13. This is something sweet, or kind of maple tree.   _____

Write on Track

Write a clue for another ord that has the sound of **s.**
Exchange clues with a cla smate.

Review

Complete each line of the poem by **writing** a word from the box. Use the sound clues to help you.

cider	gold	cold	reason	sure
Large	Pencils	season	Sugar	said

Best Time of Year

Autumn is my favorite _____.
(s in **sun**, s in **hose**)

Let me tell you just one _____.
(s in **hose**)

Even though my nose gets _____,
(c in **corn**)

I like leaves that turn to _____.
(g in **goat**)

_____ maples turn to red,
(ss in **tissue**)

_____ geese fly overhead.
(g in **giraffe**)

I love _____, turkey, too,
(c in **celery**)

_____, notebooks, all brand new.
(c in **celery**)

Oops! I _____ I'd tell just one.
(s in **sun**)

That's _____ hard. Fall's so much fun.
(ss in **tissue**)

 **Write on Track**

Name your favorite season and write a sentence or rhyme to tell why you like it best.

 PHONICS ALIVE AT HOME Ask your child to read each sound clue and then the word he or she wrote in the blank.

Name _____

Here's a Hint! S can stand for more than one sound.

sun   hose   ti**ss**ue

Say the name of the picture. **Circle** the words that have the same **s** sound as the picture name.

1.	soccer rose seven bus	**2.**	cheese his sun pies	**3.**	sugar same hose daisy
4.	yes soon was grass	**5.**	soap gas tissue sure	**6.**	music sand busy peas

Write the word from above that fits each clue.

7. This is a team sport played in the fall. _____

8. This is what you use to water the garden. _____

9. This is how you feel when you know the answer. _____

10. This is the number of days in a week. _____

11. This is the sound made when you sing. _____

12. This is what you use when you have a cold. _____

13. This is something sweet, or a kind of maple tree. _____

Write on Track

Write a clue for another word that has the sound of **s.**
Exchange clues with a classmate.

Complete each line of the poem by **writing** a word from the box. Use the sound clues to help you.

cider	gold	cold	reason	sure
Large	Pencils	season	Sugar	said

Best Time of Year

Autumn is my favorite _____.
(s in **sun**, s in **hose**)

Let me tell you just one _____.
(s in **hose**)

Even though my nose gets _____,
(c in **corn**)

I like leaves that turn to _____.
(g in **goat**)

_____ maples turn to red,
(ss in **tissue**)

_____ geese fly overhead.
(g in **giraffe**)

I love _____, turkey, too,
(c in **celery**)

_____, notebooks, all brand new.
(c in **celery**)

Oops! I _____ I'd tell just one.
(s in **sun**)

That's _____ hard. Fall's so much fun.
(ss in **tissue**)

Write on Track

Name your favorite season and write a sentence or rhyme to tell why you like it best.

PHONICS ALIVE AT HOME   Ask your child to read each sound clue and then the word he or she wrote in the blank.

Name _____

Spell, Write, and Tell

Read the phrases in the box. **Say** and **spell** each word in **bold** print. **Repeat** the word. Then **sort** the words according to sound and spelling. Two words can be listed under more than one heading.

yellow school **bus**

busy squirrels

old log **cabin**

tasty apple **cider**

cool fall nights

silly **goose**

large honking birds

brand new **pencil**

a good **reason**

seven days a week

sweet as **sugar**

sure about the answer

wagon for a hayride

fly in a **wedge**

c in **celery**	**c** in **corn**
_____	_____
_____	_____

g in **giraffe**	**g** in **goat**
_____	_____
_____	_____
	_____

s in **sun**	**s** in **hose**
_____	_____
_____	_____
_____	

s in **tissue**

_____

_____

Spell, Write, and Tell

Imagine that a spaceship has landed nearby in a pile of autumn leaves. **Write** a paragraph in which you explain autumn to the visitors from space. Begin with a topic sentence that tells the main idea, and use one or more of the words in the box. **Share** your paragraph with the class.

bus	busy	cabin	cider	cool	goose	large
pencil	reason	seven	sugar	sure	wagon	wedge

All About Autumn

PHONICS ALIVE AT HOME

Ask your child to read his or her paragraph to you and point out the words from the box that he or she used.

Name_____

Read and Write

Read the story. **Think** about what happens and try to figure out why. Then **answer** the questions.

The Bird Feeder Mystery

It was a beautiful fall day. Bonnie looked through her window at the trees in her backyard. The leaves had changed to orange and yellow and red.

A bird feeder hung down on a string from one tree branch. Bonnie had made it from a milk carton. Many different birds were fluttering around the feeder and eating the seeds. Some seeds dropped to the ground, where a large gray squirrel gobbled them up.

Bonnie smiled, pleased that the birds liked her feeder. She turned away from the window. A moment later, she heard a noise outside. When Bonnie looked back out, the bird feeder was gone!

1. What do you think happened to the bird feeder in Bonnie's backyard?

_____

_____

2. What clue helped you figure out what happened?

_____

_____

Phonics and Writing

Have you ever watched squirrels playing tag? Did you notice a dog or a cat by watching them? Do some animal watching. Then **record** what you see. Use one or more words from the box.

Writer's Tips

- Tell where and when you went animal watching.
- Describe both the place and what the animal did as you watched.
- Be as specific as you can. Tell what you saw. Tell what you heard.

autumn	calm	certain	garden	gentle	huge
leaf	roam	robin	season	warm	winter

_____

_____

_____

_____

_____

_____

_____

_____

_____

_____

Lesson 7 • Writing Consonants and Consonant Variants in Context • Comprehension: Making Inferences

PHONICS ALIVE AT HOME Ask your child to read his or her nature log to you. Together, add an entry to the log.

Name _____

READ

Let's **read** and **talk** about migrating animals.

Learn About Migrating Animals

As the days in the fall get shorter and colder, many animals get ready for winter. Some store food. Others move to a different location.

Would you choose Alaska as a winter vacation spot? Bald eagles do. Every year about three thousand of them visit the state's Chilkat River. Many salmon swim there because the water is still warm. The eagles enjoy feasting on these fish.

Many other animals choose warm, sunny places. Some monarch butterflies fly to southern California in the middle of October and gather in large groups. They hang together on tree trunks or large branches and do not move again until spring.

What do you think migrating animals do in the spring?

Check-Up **Say** the name of the picture. **Fill in** the circle next to the consonant or consonants that complete the picture name.

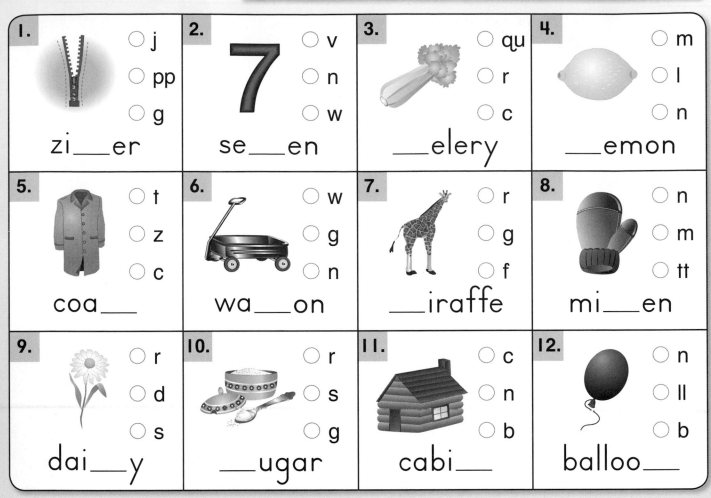

1.
○ j
○ pp
○ g
zi___er

2.
○ v
○ n
○ w
se___en

3.
○ qu
○ r
○ c
___elery

4.
○ m
○ l
○ n
___emon

5.
○ t
○ z
○ c
coa___

6.
○ w
○ g
○ n
wa___on

7.
○ r
○ g
○ f
___iraffe

8.
○ n
○ m
○ tt
mi___en

9.
○ r
○ d
○ s
dai___y

10.
○ r
○ s
○ g
___ugar

11.
○ c
○ n
○ b
cabi___

12.
○ n
○ ll
○ b
balloo___

Check-Up **Fill in** the circle next to the word that makes sense in each sentence.

13. September marks the beginning of ___. ○ August ○ autumn

14. Each ___ day is a little shorter. ○ far ○ fall

15. The ___ sets a little earlier. ○ sum ○ sun

16. The air feels ___. ○ pool ○ cool

17. Green leaves turn ___ and red. ○ yellow ○ fellow

18. A ___ stores twigs and sticks. ○ beaver ○ beeper

19. The ___ ends in December. ○ reason ○ season

PHONICS ALIVE AT HOME Review this Check-Up with your child.

SONG

Sing to the sun
It will listen
And warm your words
Your joy will rise
Like the sun
And glow
Within you

Sing to the moon
It will hear
And soothe your cares
Your fears will set
Like the moon
And fade
Within you

Ashley Bryan

Critical Thinking Why would you sing a song to the sun? to the moon?
How does the moon's response differ from the sun's response?

PHONICS ALIVE AT HOME

Name _____

Dear Family,

As your child reviews the short and long vowel sounds of **a, i, o, u,** and **e,** he or she will read about ways in which music enriches our lives.

• Say each word below and listen for the short or long vowel sound.

Apreciada Familia,

A medida que los niños repasan los sonidos cortos y largos de las vocales, **a, i, o, u, e,** leerán acerca de como la música enriquece nuestras vidas.

• Pronuncien las siguientes palabras y escuchen el sonido corto o largo en cada una.

short **a**	short **i**	short **o**	short **u**	short **e**
b<u>a</u>nd	d<u>i</u>sk	p<u>o</u>nd	dr<u>u</u>m	s<u>e</u>nd

long **a**	long **i**	long **o**	long **u**	long **e**
g<u>ai</u>n	f<u>i</u>ve	n<u>o</u>te	s<u>ui</u>t	f<u>ee</u>t

• Read the poem on the reverse side. Talk about "sun songs" and "moon songs."

• Read the first stanza of the poem again. Ask your child to read the second stanza.

• Look for short and long vowel words in the poem.

• Lean el poema en la página 21. Hablen de canciones acerca del sol y la luna.

• De nuevo lea la primera estrofa del poema. Pida al niño leer la segunda estrofa.

• Busquen en el poema palabras con vocales de sonidos cortos y largos.

PROJECT

Have a sing-along with your child. Sing a few songs. Then write down the titles or the words to the songs. Help your child circle each word with a short vowel sound and underline each word with a long vowel sound.

Strike Up the Band

Blue Skies

PROYECTO

Prepare una tarde de cantos junto con el niño. Canten varias canciones. Después escriban los títulos o las palabras de las canciones. Encierren en un círculo las palabras con vocales de sonido corto y subrayen las palabras con vocales de sonido largo.

 Visit us at **www.sadlierphonicsonline.com**

**Here's
a Hint!** If there are two vowels in a one-syllable word, the first vowel is usually **long** and the second vowel is silent.

cake   five   rope   dune   bean

Look at the different spellings for long **a**.

cake   rain   jay

Say the name of the picture. **Circle** and **write** the long **a** word that names it.
In the last box, **draw** your own long **a** picture. **Write** the word.

1. cake / came / cape	2. trail / tray / train	3. pay / pain / pave
4. sell / sail / sake	5. play / plate / plane	6.

Scale has the long **a** phonogram **ale**. **Say** the name of the picture.
Circle the long **a** phonogram in the picture name.

7. _al / _ale / _ate	8. _ate / _an / _ain	9. _ay / _ade / _ail
10. _ake / _ain / _ail	11. _ace / _ake / _age	12. _ain / _ame / _am
13. _ake / _ag / _age	14. _ay / _ail / _at	15. _al / _ale / _ate

Add the initial consonant to the long **a** phonogram to build a word. **Write** the word.

1. g + ain _____	2. n + ame _____
3. w + ay _____	4. f + ade _____
5. s + ave _____	6. qu + ake _____
7. d + ate _____	8. n + ail _____

Word Strategy You can use a long vowel phonogram you know to help you read an unknown word.

Write a word from the box to complete each sentence. **Read** the selection about sound.

brain	made	plays	say	shake	take	wave

How is sound _____? Let's _____

Gail sings a note. When she sings, she makes the

air vibrate, or _____. The shaking air moves

in a _____ until it reaches Jay's ear. Before

long, Jay's _____ makes sense of the sound.

What if Gail _____ a violin?

When she plucks the strings, the air vibrates.

It doesn't _____ long for Jay to hear music.

Write on Track Suppose a tree falls in the forest, but no one is there to hear it. Does the tree still make a sound? Write what you think.

PHONICS ALIVE AT HOME Ask your child to sort the words in the box by spelling pattern: a_e, ai, ay.

Name _____

Look at the different spellings for long **i**.
f**i**ve   t**ie**   l**igh**t   w**i**nd
Say the name of the picture. **Write** the long **i** word from the box that names it.
In the last box, **draw** your own long **i** picture. **Write** the word.

bike	five	knight	lime	pie	rind	smile

1. 5

_____

2.

_____

3.

_____

4.

_____

5.

_____

6.

_____

7.

_____

8.

_____

Slide has the long **i** phonogram **ide**. **Say** the name of the picture. **Circle** the long **i** phonogram in the picture name. **Write** the phonogram to complete the word.

9.
__id
__ed
__ide
sl_____

10.
__ie
__ile
__ide
t_____

11.
__igh
__ight
__it
l_____

12.
__in
__ind
__ine
w_____

13.
__ice
__ipe
__ise
r_____

14.
__ike
__ane
__ine
p_____

Phonics in Context

Work Together Read each word. **Write** a word with the same long **i** phonogram. **Compare** answers with a partner.

1. mind _____	2. ripe _____	3. night _____
4. line _____	5. mile _____	6. nice _____
7. bike _____	8. hive _____	9. pie _____

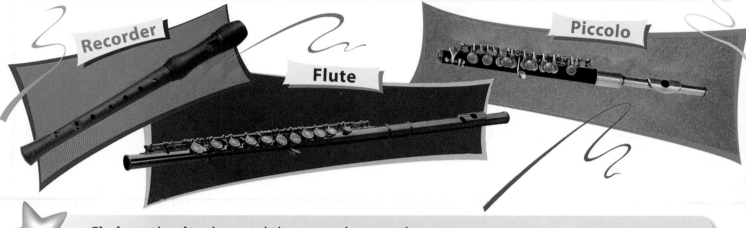

Recorder

Flute

Piccolo

Circle and **write** the word that completes each sentence.

10. You might _____ a pipe under a sink.   find   fine

11. You also _____ check a band.   might   right

12. A pipe is a _____ of musical instrument.   kid   kind

13. A recorder is a _____ that is made from wood.   pie   pipe

14. It is _____ to carry and easy to play.   light   lie

15. A flute is a pipe that sounds _____ a bird.   lick   like

16. Hold it to the _____ to play a tune.   ride   side

17. To hit the _____ notes, play the piccolo.   high   hike

18. It's a flute that is the _____ of a ruler.   rise   size

19. I will listen _____ you play.   white   while

PHONICS ALIVE AT HOME With your child, look for long **i** words in a newspaper, magazine, or book.

Look at the different spellings for long **o**.

rope   boat   snow   hoe   gold

Say the name of the picture. **Circle** and **write** the long **o** word that names it.
In the last box, **draw** your own long **o** picture. **Write** the word.

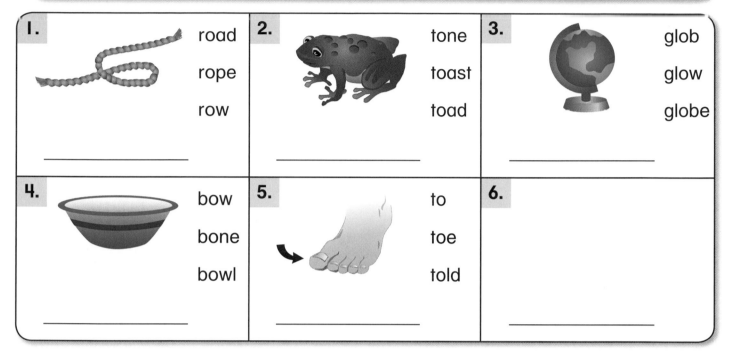

1.   road   rope   row   _____

2.   tone   toast   toad   _____

3.   glob   glow   globe   _____

4.   bow   bone   bowl   _____

5.   to   toe   told   _____

6.   _____

Cone has the long **o** phonogram **one**. **Say** the name of the picture. **Say** the long **o** phonogram in the picture name. **Circle** the words with the same phonogram.

7.   lone   man   zone   tone   **cone**

8.   coat   bat   goat   plot   **boat**

9.   foam   soak   glow   grow   **snow**

10.   hole   toe   doe   toad   **hoe**

11.   fold   bow   gold   grow   **mow**

12.   slope   spoke   woke   soap   **smoke**

Work Together

Work with a partner. **Write** a long **o** word from the box to answer each question.

colt	go	home	mow	note	throat	toast	toe

1. What is a musical sound that you sing? _____

2. What is a young horse? _____

3. What is the opposite of **stay?** _____

4. What means about the same as **cut?** _____

5. What is the front of the neck? _____

6. What goes well with jam? _____

7. What is another word for **house?** _____

8. What is the opposite of **heel?** _____

blow	bow	cold	doe	groan	low	pole	tone

9. What do you hear when you pick up the phone? _____

10. What is a female deer? _____

11. What is the opposite of **hot?** _____

12. What do you use for fishing? _____

13. What means about the same as **moan?** _____

14. What do you use to play a violin? _____

15. What is the opposite of **high?** _____

16. How do you play the flute? _____

Write on Track

Write two or three questions that can be answered with long **o** words. Exchange questions with a classmate.

PHONICS ALIVE AT HOME With your child, take turns reading the questions and answers on the page.

Name _____

Look at the different spellings for long **u**.
     d**u**ne   s**ui**t   bl**ue**
Say the name of the picture. **Circle** and **write** the long **u** word that names it.
In the last box, **draw** your own long **u** picture. **Write** the word.

1.
den
due
dune
_____

2.
glum
glue
blue
_____

3.
lute
tub
tube
_____

4.
July
Jane
June
_____

5.
fruit
fuse
flute
_____

6.
_____

June has the long **u** phonogram **une**. **Say** the name of the picture. **Say** the long **u** phonogram in the picture name. **Circle** the words with the same phonogram.

7.
dune
June
plume
prune
dude
tune

8.
sigh
Sue
fruit
use
true
suit

9.
huge
clue
glue
play
due
blue

10.
smile
rule
sale
male
yule
mule

11.
rude
fuse
tub
tube
fuss
cube

12.
cute
flat
flight
fume
lute
flute

Word Strategy You can use a long vowel phonogram you know to help you read an unknown word.

The blues are a kind of song that you sing when you are sad. **Read** the titles of some unusual blues songs. **Circle** and **write** the long **u** words. **Add** two titles of your own to the list.

1. My Glue Won't Stick _____

2. The Runaway Mule _____

3. The Melted Ice Cube _____

4. Don't Know the Rules _____

5. Can't Keep a Tune _____

6. Can't Stand That Green Suit _____

7. Ate Rotten Fruit _____

8. Miss My Friend Sue _____

9. Don't Have a Clue _____

10. Can't Squeeze the Tube _____

11. Don't Own a Flute _____

12. My Cat Is Rude _____

13. I've Got the Blues _____

14. _____

    _____

15. _____

    _____

Write on Track Choose one title. Work with a classmate and write the lyrics, or words, to the song.

PHONICS ALIVE AT HOME Ask your child to use long **u** words to make up titles for songs to sing when you are happy.

Name _____

Spell, Write, and Tell

Read the phrases in the box. **Say** and **spell** each word in **bold** print. **Repeat** the word. **Sort** the words according to sound and spelling.

feel the **beat**

ring a **bell**

clap your hands

stamp your **feet**

hop like a bunny

hum a tune

last in **line**

hit a high **note**

turn to the **right**

shake, rattle, and roll

sing a song

wear a western **suit**

heel and **toe**

go this **way**

Short Vowels

a _____

i _____

o _____

u _____

e _____

Long Vowels

a _____

_____

i _____

_____

o _____

_____

u _____

e _____

_____

Spelling and Writing

Write a paragraph that tells how to sing a song, do a dance, or play an instrument. Use time order words, such as **first, next, then,** and one or more of the words in the box. See if a friend can follow your directions.

beat	bell	clap	feet	hop	hum	line
note	right	shake	sing	suit	toe	way

_____

_____

_____

_____

_____

_____

_____

_____

_____

44

Lesson 20 • Connecting Spelling, Writing, and Speaking

 PHONICS ALIVE AT HOME

Ask your child to read his or her paragraph to you and to point out the time order words.

Name _____

Read and Write **Read** the true story about a great musician.
Think about the main idea. **Answer** the questions.

MOZART: The Musical Wonder Child

At age four, he played the keyboard. At age five, he began to write music. At age six, he performed for an emperor! Who is he? Wolfgang Amadeus Mozart— a musical wonder child.

Mozart was born in Austria in 1756 into a musical family. His father Leopold, a famous musician, soon became his teacher. Leopold taught young Mozart to play the harpsichord and the violin. Amazed by his son's talent, Leopold decided to go on a concert tour.

Leopold took Mozart all over Europe. The family visited Vienna, Paris, and London—all before Mozart was ten years old. On tour, Mozart played three instruments. He had his first music published, and he wrote his first opera.

As Mozart grew older, he kept writing music. He wrote over 600 pieces during his lifetime. You can still hear them today.

1. Who was Mozart's music teacher?

_____

_____

2. What was amazing about young Mozart? List two things.

_____

_____

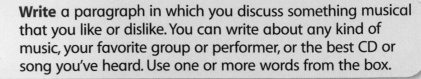

Phonics and Writing

Write a paragraph in which you discuss something musical that you like or dislike. You can write about any kind of music, your favorite group or performer, or the best CD or song you've heard. Use one or more words from the box.

Writer's Tips

- Start by telling what you will discuss. Tell what you like or dislike about it.
- Give at least two reasons for your likes and dislikes.

amaze	best	dance	least	play	smile
band	blast	excite	music	rock	tune

Lesson 21 • Writing Short and Long Vowels in Context
Comprehension: Recognizing Main Idea and Details

Ask your child to read his or her paragraph to you. Discuss your taste in music with your child.

Name _____

Let's **read** and **talk** about a famous ballet.

Learn About a Ballet

Have you ever seen a ballet? In this kind of performance, dancers and music help tell a story.

The Nutcracker is one of the world's most popular ballets. The main character is a girl named Clara, who receives a gift of a wooden doll that can crack nuts with its teeth. When the Nutcracker comes alive, he and Clara have many adventures. They fight with a mouse called the Mouse King. They see dancing snowflakes. They also meet the Sugar Plum Fairy and travel to the Land of Sweets.

Are Clara and the Nutcracker's adventures real, or are they part of a dream? To find out, read the story of the Nutcracker. Or, if possible, watch a performance.

What story would you like to see performed as a ballet? Tell the story in your own words.

Lesson 22 • Short and Long Vowels in Context
Comprehension: Summarizing
Developing Fluency

47

8/20/2[...]

Say the name of the picture. **Fill in** the circle next to the word that names it.

I.
- ○ bird
- ◉ band
- ○ bond

2.
- ○ pin
- ○ pain
- ◉ pine

3.
- ◉ cub
- ○ cube
- ○ cute

4.
- ○ tray
- ◉ train
- ○ trade

5.
- ○ stamp
- ○ stomp
- ◉ stop

6.
- ○ will
- ○ while
- ◉ well

7.
- ○ hay
- ○ he
- ◉ hoe

8.
- ○ fright
- ◉ fruit
- ○ frame

9.
- ○ fan
- ◉ fin
- ○ fine

10.
- ◉ team
- ○ tame
- ○ tea

II.
- ○ vet
- ○ vote
- ◉ vest

12.
- ◉ bone
- ○ bold
- ○ boat

Underline each word with a long vowel sound. **Write yes** or **no** to answer the question.

13. Can a huge whale play notes on a scale?

14. Is a dime the same size as a lime?

15. Can you bend your knees and tap your toes?

16. Can you squeeze a tube to get glue?

17. Is a green leaf the same as a red jet?

18. Can you use a mug to drink milk with a meal?

NO

NO
YES
YES
NO
YES

PHONICS ALIVE AT HOME — Review this Check-Up with your child.

Sunflakes

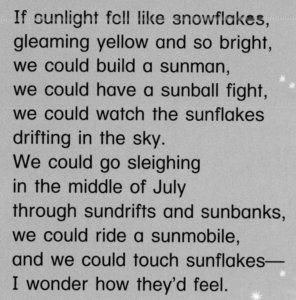

If sunlight fell like snowflakes,
gleaming yellow and so bright,
we could build a sunman,
we could have a sunball fight,
we could watch the sunflakes
drifting in the sky.
We could go sleighing
in the middle of July
through sundrifts and sunbanks,
we could ride a sunmobile,
and we could touch sunflakes—
I wonder how they'd feel.

Frank Asch

Critical Thinking If sunlight fell like snowflakes, what would you do?
If you could touch sunflakes, how do you think they would feel?

Lesson 23 • Syllables, Consonant Blends, Compound Words,
y as a Vowel, Silent Letters, and Consonant Digraphs
Poetry: Rhythm and Rhyme
Developing Fluency

49

Dear Family,

In this unit your child will use his or her imagination while learning phonics skills. Share these definitions:

> **consonant blend:** two or three consonants sounded together so that each letter is heard (**cl**oud, ne**st**)
>
> **compound word:** a word made up of two or more smaller words (**sunlight**)
>
> **words with y as a vowel:** words in which **y** has the sound of long **i** or long **e** (sh**y**, part**y**)
>
> **consonant digraph:** two consonants together that stand for one sound (**th**ink, wi**sh**)
>
> **silent letter:** a letter that appears in a word but whose sound is not said (**g**nat)

- Read the poem on the reverse side, emphasizing the rhyming words. Talk about what would happen if sunlight fell like snowflakes.

- Look in the poem for examples of consonant blends, compound words, words with **y** as a vowel, and consonant digraphs.

Apreciada Familia,

En esta unidad los niños usarán la imaginación mientras aprenden destrezas fonéticas. Compartan estas definiciones:

> **mezcla de consonantes:** dos o tres consonantes se combinan de manera que cada una se puede oír (**cl**oud, ne**st**)
>
> **palabras compuestas:** una palabra formada por dos o más palabras (**sunlight**)
>
> **y con sonido de vocal:** palabras donde la **y** tiene el sonido largo de la **i** o la **e** (sh**y**, part**y**)
>
> **consonantes dígrafas:** dos consonantes juntas que producen un solo sonido (**th**ink, wi**sh**)
>
> **letra muda:** letra que aparece en una palabra pero no se pronuncia (**g**nat)

- Lea el poema en la página 49 pausando después de cada par de versos para reforzar las palabras rítmicas. Hablen de lo que pasaría si la luz solar cayera como copos de nieve.

- Busquen ejemplos en el poema de mezcla de consonantes, palabras compuestas, palabras donde la **y** tiene sonido vocal y consonantes dígrafas.

PROJECT

With your child, make a list of compound words. Write each word part on an index card. Shuffle the cards and pick two at random to make a new compound word. Use the word in a silly sentence.

PROYECTO

Hagan una lista de palabras compuestas. Escriban las partes de las palabras en una tarjeta 3 X 5. Barajen las tarjetas y saquen dos para formar una nueva palabra compuesta con ellas. Usen la palabra en una oración tonta.

50 **Lesson 23** • Syllables, Consonant Blends, Compound Words, **y** as a Vowel, Silent Letters, and Consonant Digraphs—Phonics Alive at Home

 Visit us at **www.sadlierphonicsonline.com**

Name _____

Here's a Hint! A **consonant blend** is two or three consonants sounded together so that each letter is heard.
cloud **tw**ig **dr**um **sn**ow ne**st**

Say the name of the picture. **Circle** the blend that begins each picture name. **Write** an **l** blend or **tw** to complete the word. In the last box, **draw** your own **l** blend or **tw** picture. **Write** the word.

1. pl cl gl ___aw	**2.** sl fl tw ___oat	**3.** tw pl bl ___enty
4. gl sl fl ___obe	**5.** tr tw wr ___ig	**6.** _____

Read each word. **Write** a word with the same phonogram. Begin the new word with a blend from the box.

bl	cl	fl	gl	pl	sl	tw

7. sock _____	**8.** tub _____
9. bat _____	**10.** dig _____
11. red _____	**12.** name _____
13. bow _____	**14.** gate _____

Drum begins with the **r** blend **dr**. **Say** the name of the picture. **Write** an **r** blend to complete the word. Then **draw** your own **r** blend picture. **Write** the word.

br	cr	dr	fr	gr	pr	tr

1. ___awl

2. ___idge

3. ___ain

4. ___aph

5. ___uit

6. ___ess

7. ___ize

8. _____

Write a word from the box to complete each sentence.

drum	crab	truck	frame	brave

9. The _____ ran out of the water and into a hole in the sand.

10. My mom bought a _____ and put my picture in it.

11. The pounding of the _____ could be heard for miles.

12. The bright green _____ got a flat tire on the highway.

13. The _____ prince chased away the dragon.

Write on Track

Make up a story using one of the words from the word box as the topic. Write the story.

PHONICS ALIVE AT HOME

With your child, make up a sentence with three **r** blend words. For example: The **dragon** under the **bridge breathes** fire.

Word Strategy You can use a syllable you know to help you read an unknown word.

cat   clatter   flatter   platter   scatter

 Say each syllable. Combine the syllables to **write** a word.

1.

clat + ter   _____

flat + ter   _____

plat + ter   _____

scat + ter   _____

2.

squeak + y   _____

sneak + y   _____

creak + y   _____

streak + y   _____

3.

play + ing   _____

stay + ing   _____

spray + ing   _____

bray + ing   _____

4.

land + ed   _____

hand + ed   _____

sand + ed   _____

brand + ed   _____

 Work Together Write the two-syllable word from above that fits each clue. **Compare** answers with a partner.

5. It begins with **clat.**
It's another word for **noise.**

The word is _____.

6. It begins with **stay.**
It's the opposite of **going.**

The word is _____.

7. It begins with **creak.**
It describes a door that needs oil.

The word is _____.

8. It begins with **hand.**
It's another word for **gave.**

The word is _____.

9. It begins with **sand.**
It means "made smooth."

The word is _____.

10. It begins with **plat.**
It's a large dish.

The word is _____.

Assessment

Check-Up Say the name of the picture. **Write** the word that names it. **Circle** the consonant blend at the beginning or end of the picture name.

1.	2.	3.	4.
_____	_____	_____	_____

5.	6.	7.	8.
_____	_____	_____	_____

9.	10.	11.	12.
_____	_____	_____	_____

Check-Up Circle the word that fits each clue.

13.	This is used for cooking or heating.	store	grove	stove
14.	This is another word for **noise.**	cloud	sound	found
15.	This is where birds lay eggs.	nest	vest	tent
16.	This strong string can be used to tie boxes.	twine	spine	swine
17.	This word goes with **ice.**	snail	snow	stow
18.	This is used to stick things together.	blue	glue	clue
19.	This is used for cooking or broiling.	drill	skill	grill
20.	This instrument makes a sound when you beat it.	plum	drum	spun

PHONICS ALIVE AT HOME Review this Check-Up with your child.

Name _____

Here's a Hint! A compound word is made up of two or more smaller words.

wish + bone = wishbone

 Combine two words from the box to name the picture. **Write** the compound word. In the last box, **draw** your own compound word picture. **Write** the word.

back	ball	bone	box	coat	foot	lace
mail	mill	pack	rain	shoe	wind	wish

1.	**2.**	**3.**	**4.**
_____	_____	_____	_____
5.	**6.**	**7.**	**8.**
_____	_____	_____	_____

 Work Together **Write** a compound word from above for each definition. Take turns **reading** the definitions and compound words with a partner.

9. This is a ball you kick with your foot. _____

10. This is a bone you make a wish on. _____

11. This is a lace used to tie a shoe. _____

12. This is a coat that protects you from rain. _____

13. This is a mill that is worked by the wind. _____

14. This is a pack you wear on your back. _____

15. This is a box in which you mail letters. _____

Add a word from the box to each word to form a compound word. **Write** the compound word.

cut	flake	fruit	hive	lid
side	stairs	time	way	work

1. snow _____	**2.** hill _____
3. hair _____	**4.** bed _____
5. grape _____	**6.** home _____
7. eye _____	**8.** up _____
9. drive _____	**10.** bee _____

 Word Strategy You can use a syllable or small word you know to help you read a compound word.

 Read each sentence and **circle** the compound word. Use the word clues to help you.

rain   **11.** What kind of flakes would fall from a rainbow?

box   **12.** Look what I found in my mailbox!

pan   **13.** Why is our kitchen filled with pancakes?

ship   **14.** Is that a spaceship in the yard?

fish   **15.** That is the strangest goldfish I've ever seen!

play   **16.** Did you ever have a make-believe playmate?

 Write on Track How many compound words can you make by adding a word after **snow**? before **ball**? Make a list with a classmate.

PHONICS ALIVE AT HOME With your child, take turns making up definitions for the compound words circled in items 11–16.

Name _____

Here's a Hint! **Y** usually has the long **i** sound when it is the only vowel at the end of a one-syllable word. When **y** is the only vowel at the end of a word with more than one syllable, it usually has the long **e** sound.

fl**y**—**1** syllable—long **i**   b**a**b**y**—**2** syllables—long **e**

Say the words in the box. **Write** the words in which **y** has the long **i** sound under the fly. **Write** the words in which **y** has the long **e** sound under the baby.

by	cry	daisy	jelly	muddy
my	penny	puppy	sky	spy

I.

Long i

_____

_____

_____

_____

2.

Long e

_____

_____

_____

_____

Write a word from above to complete each question.

3. Why is the _____ blue and the grass green?

4. Why won't a _____ stay shiny?

5. Why does peanut butter go with _____?

6. Why does a _____ try to eat slippers?

7. Why does a baby _____ at night and sleep during the day?

8. Why does it rain when I forget _____ umbrella?

Syllables

Word Strategy You can use what you know about syllables to help you read words that end in **y.**

Read each phrase. **Write** the number of syllables you hear in the word that ends in **y.** **Write Long i** if the **y** has the long **i** sound. **Write Long e** if the **y** has the long **e** sound.

	Number of Syllables	Vowel Sound of **y**
1. ask **why**	_____	_____
2. a **funny** joke	_____	_____
3. a **happy** smile	_____	_____
4. **sly** as a fox	_____	_____
5. **my** best friend	_____	_____
6. go **slowly**	_____	_____
7. **easy** as can be	_____	_____
8. **many** years ago	_____	_____
9. **fry** an egg	_____	_____
10. **fly** a kite	_____	_____
11. a **pretty** face	_____	_____
12. on **dry** land	_____	_____
13. **carry** an umbrella	_____	_____
14. **try** harder	_____	_____

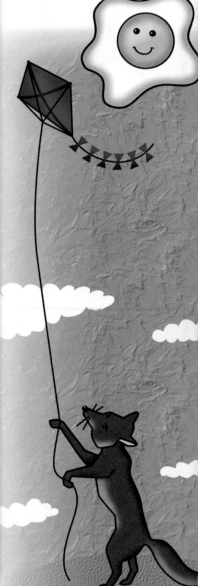

Write a sentence using two or more words that end in **y.** Go back and **circle** each two-syllable word that ends in **y.**

_____

_____

PHONICS ALIVE AT HOME Together, look for words with **y** as a vowel in a newspaper, magazine, or book. Say the words.

Name _____

Digraphs

Here's a Hint! A **consonant digraph** is two consonants together that stand for one sound.

think   clo**ck**   di**sh**es

Say the name of the picture. **Circle** the consonant digraph that begins each picture name. **Write** the digraph to complete the word.

1. ___ink — ch / sh / th	2. ___air — wr / ch / th	3. ___ip — kn / wh / sh
4. ___umb — th / wr / ch	5. ___eat — wh / wr / sh	6. ___eck — sh / th / ch
7. ___eel — sh / wh / th	8. ___ed — ch / sh / wh	9. ___ell — th / sh / wh

---

Write a word from the box to complete each sentence.

child	when	share	think	What	short

10. _____ would it be like to be a chair?

11. Does a chair _____ it is useful?

12. A _____ can sit and read in a cozy chair.

13. Two friends can _____ a seat.

14. A child can settle in for a _____ nap.

15. What does a chair do _____ it is tired?

Lesson 34 • Recognizing and Writing Initial Consonant Digraphs **th, sh, wh, ch**

69

Copyright © by William H. Sadlier, Inc. All rights reserved.

Consonant Digraphs

Clock ends with the consonant digraph **ck**. **Say** the name of the picture. **Write** the word that names each one.

beach	brush	chick	clock	couch	dish
fish	moth	peach	teeth	tooth	truck

I. _____

2. _____

3. _____

4. _____

5. _____

6. _____

7. _____

8. _____

9. _____

10. _____

11. _____

12. _____

Work Together Work with a partner. **Write** a word from above to complete each rhyme.

13. If I were a _____,
I'd tick and I'd tock.

14. If I were a _____,
I'd find a worm quick.

15. If I were a _____,
I'd swim and I'd swish.

16. If I were a _____,
I'd often say "Ouch!"

17. If I were a _____,
I'd eat holes in cloth.

18. If I were a _____,
I'd stay out of reach.

70 Lesson 34 • Recognizing and Writing Final Consonant Digraphs **ck, th, sh, ch**

Ask your child to sort the words in the box by final consonant digraph: **ck, th, sh, ch.**

Dishes has the consonant digraph **sh** in the middle. **Say** the name of the picture. **Circle** its consonant digraph. **Write** the digraph to complete the word.

1.		2.		3.	
	sh th ch		sh ch ck		th wh sh
di__es		ni__el		fea__er	

4.		5.		6.	
	ck ch th		sh wh th		ch ck sh
pea__es		pin__eel		bu__el	

7.		8.		9.	
	th ck sh		sh ch ck		ch th wh
che__ers		bu__le		arm__air	

Read the travel ad. **Underline** each word that has a consonant digraph in the middle. **Circle** the digraph.

Visit the enchanted
Island of Friendship!

Sit awhile in the sunshine. Have fun splashing in the warm water.
Go somewhere interesting every day . . . or relax and do nothing.
Purchase a ticket quickly!
This trip makes a great birthday gift.

Write on Track

Imagine visiting this enchanted island. Write a postcard home.

Here's a Hint! The consonant digraphs **ph** and **gh** can stand for the same sound.

phone   cou**gh**

Say the name of the picture. **Write** the word that names each one.

cough	dolphin	elephant	graph
laugh	phone	photo	trophy

1.
_____

2.
_____

3.
_____

4.
_____

5.
_____

6.
_____

7.
_____

8.
_____

Circle each word that has the consonant digraph **ph** or **gh**.
Write yes or no to answer the question.

9. Can you make a phone call?   _____

10. Does clean air make you cough?   _____

11. Are most elephants tiny?   _____

12. Do you laugh at funny jokes?   _____

13. Can you hear a photo?   _____

14. Can a dolphin draw a graph?   _____

15. Is tree bark rough?   _____

16. Is a trophy a prize?   _____

PHONICS ALIVE AT HOME   Together, make up additional questions using the words in the box above.

Word Strategy You can use a syllable you know to help you read an unknown word.

chat   chatter   chatty

Say each syllable. Combine the syllables to **write** a word.

1. chat + ter _____		**2.** sharp + en _____	
chat + ty _____		sharp + er _____	
3. thir + ty _____		**4.** wrap + per _____	
thir + teen _____		wrap + ping _____	
5. pho + to _____		**6.** teach + er _____	
pho + ny _____		teach + es _____	
7. quick + ly _____		**8.** fish + ing _____	
quick + est _____		fish + y _____	

Work Together **Write** the two-syllable word from above that fits each clue. Take turns **reading** the clues and answers with a partner.

9. It begins with **teach.**
It's someone who gives lessons.

The word is _____.

10. It begins with **pho.**
It's another word for **fake.**

The word is _____.

11. It begins with **fish.**
It describes how something smells.

The word is _____.

12. It begins with **sharp.**
It's what you do to a pencil.

The word is _____.

13. It begins with **quick.**
It's another word for **fastest.**

The word is _____.

14. It begins with **thir.**
It's one more than twelve.

The word is _____.

 Read about Rough Tough Phill. **Answer** the questions.

Rough Tough Phill

Rough Tough Phill was the biggest, strongest person in Wheelbarrow County. She could carry an elephant under her arm. She could ride a whale clear across the ocean and back. She could eat thirty bushels of peaches at one sitting.

One day Phill heard about The Strongest Person on Earth Contest. It was being held in Cherrytown, 7,629 miles away. Nothing would stop Phill from entering the contest and winning the trophy.

Phill set out for Cherrytown. She charged down the path like a herd of bulls. People heard thunder as Phill passed by. Boom! Crack! Crash!

I. Who was Rough Tough Phill?

_____

2. Why did she set out for Cherrytown?

_____

3. What do you think is the most amazing thing that Phill could do?

_____

_____

4. What do you think happens next in the story?

_____

_____

_____

_____

PHONICS ALIVE AT HOME Ask your child to read "Rough Tough Phill" to you. Make up an ending for the story.

Spell, Write, and Tell **Read** the phrases in the box. **Say** and **spell** each word in **bold** print. **Repeat** the word. **Sort** the words according to sound and spelling. One word can be listed under more than one heading.

the **crash** of thunder

a pretty **photo**

a happy **laugh**

two for a **nickel**

nothing to do

phone home

shiny new pennies

somewhere over the rainbow

a **south** wind

warm **sunshine**

a **thick** fog

touch snowflakes

when it began to rain

a **rough** ride

Initial Consonant Digraphs

th _____

sh _____

wh _____

ph _____

_____

Final Consonant Digraphs

ck _____

th _____

sh _____

ch _____

gh _____

_____

Medial Consonant Digraphs

sh _____

ck _____

th _____

wh _____

Spell, Write, and Tell Imagine that one day it rains cornflakes, pennies, or something else. **Write** a journal entry in which you describe the unusual weather and tell how you spent the day. In your entry, use one or more of the words in the box. **Present** your writing to classmates.

crash	photo	laugh	nickel	nothing	phone	shiny
somewhere	south	sunshine	thick	touch	when	rough

Date: _____

_____

_____

_____

_____

_____

_____

_____

_____

_____

_____

_____

_____

PHONICS ALIVE AT HOME Ask your child to act as a weather forecaster and to present his or her journal entry to you.

Read the tall tale. **Think** about the problem that Lenny faces and how the problem is solved. **Answer** the questions.

Lenny Longlegs and the Star

Lenny Longlegs was the tallest man who ever lived. He was so tall that he could see over trees, mountains, and buildings. When he walked, clouds tickled his nose. Sometimes this made him sneeze, which caused a tornado!

One night Lenny's friend Stella asked if he could touch the stars. Lenny said, "I'll try." He reached up with his enormous arm. He stretched and stretched, but not far enough.

"Jump," Stella suggested. Lenny jumped, but he still couldn't touch the twinkling stars.

"Jump from higher up," Stella said. "From a mountaintop."

Lenny climbed to the very top of the tallest mountain in the world. He took a deep breath and leaped as high as he could. His fingers curled around a star. Lenny pulled the star out of the sky and gave it to Stella.

1. What is Lenny's problem?

_____

_____

2. How does Lenny solve the problem?

_____

_____

Write your own tall tale. **Introduce** the smallest, fastest, or strongest person in the world. **Tell** about a problem he or she faces and solves. Use one or more words from the box.

Writer's Tips

- Start by telling what is special about your main character.
- Use details. Give examples of the amazing things the character can do.
- Tell about a problem. Have your character use his or her abilities to solve the problem.

bridge	dragon	elephant	fly	nest	playground
know	ship	sleep	swim	think	twist

Lesson 40 • Writing Syllables, Consonant Blends, Compound Words, **y** as a Vowel, Silent Letters, and Consonant Digraphs in Context Comprehension: Identifying Problem/Solution

78

Ask your child to read his or her tall tale to you. Together, make up another tall tale.

READ

Let's **read** and **talk** about rainbows.

Learn About Rainbows

What do you imagine when you see a rainbow in the sky? Long ago, people thought that following a rainbow's path would make them rich. They believed they would find a pot of gold at a rainbow's end.

Today we know a rainbow is not magical. It is simply a curve or bow made by sunlight shining on drops of water. Sunlight is made up of many colors. When the sunlight shines on raindrops, it divides into blue, green, yellow, orange, red, and other colors. The raindrops reflect the colors like a mirror. So if the sun is behind you and rain is falling in front of you, you may see a rainbow in the sky.

The next time it rains, look for a rainbow. Notice where the sun is and where the rain is falling. Think about the reasons for rainbows.

How would you explain a rainbow to a friend?

Lesson 41 • Syllables, Consonant Blends, Compound Words, **y** as a Vowel, Silent Letters, and Consonant Digraphs in Context
Comprehension: Understanding Cause and Effect
Developing Fluency

79

Check-Up **Say** the name of the picture. **Write** the letters that complete each picture name.

1. too___	**2.** ___air	**3.** clo___	**4.** di___es
5. fea___er	**6.** ___ot	**7.** lau___	**8.** ni___el
9. pea___es	**10.** ___ip	**11.** ___eel	**12.** ___ist

Check-Up **Fill in** the circle next to the word that makes sense in each sentence.

13. Do you like to go to the _____?	○ leash	○ beach
14. What if you were a _____?	○ fish	○ quick
15. Do you _____ how you'd spend each day?	○ show	○ know
16. Would you like _____ in the sea?	○ splashing	○ packing
17. Would you go swimming with a _____?	○ dolphin	○ elephant
18. Or would you end up in somebody's _____?	○ dish	○ sharp
19. I _____ I'd rather be me.	○ thing	○ think

PHONICS ALIVE AT HOME Review this Check-Up with your child.

The Sidewalk Racer

Skimming
an asphalt sea
I swerve, I curve, I
sway; I speed to whirring
sound an inch above the
ground; I'm the sailor
and the sail; I'm the
driver and the wheel
I'm the one and only
single engine
human auto
mobile.

Lillian Morrison

Critical Thinking Why does the sidewalk racer call herself a sailor and a sail, a driver and a wheel, a single engine human automobile? How else could you describe a sidewalk racer?

Name _____

Dear Family,

In this unit about sports and games, your child will learn the sounds of vowel combinations. Share these definitions:

> **r-controlled vowel:** an **r** after a vowel gives the vowel a new sound (st**ar**, t**or**ch, ch**air**, sp**ear**)
>
> **vowel digraph:** two letters that come together to make a long, short, or special vowel sound (h**ea**d, s**ea**t, h**oo**k, b**oo**t)
>
> **diphthong:** two letters blended together that can stand for one vowel sound (cl**ow**n, cl**ou**d, c**oi**ns, t**oy**s, cr**ew**)

• Read the poem on the reverse side. Talk about the way the sidewalk racer moves.

• Read the poem again. Ask your child to move like the sidewalk racer as you read.

• Search through the poem for words with **r**-controlled vowels, vowel digraphs, and diphthongs.

Apreciada Familia,

En esta unidad sobre los deportes los niños aprenderán los sonidos de vocales combinadas. Compartan las siguientes definiciones:

> **vocales controladas por la r:** una **r** después de una vocal da a la vocal un nuevo sonido (st**ar**, t**or**ch, ch**air**, sp**ear**)
>
> **vocal dígrafa:** dos letras que juntas hacen un sonido vocal largo, corto o especial (h**ea**d, s**ea**t, h**oo**k, b**oo**t)
>
> **diptongo:** dos letras que juntas producen un solo sonido vocal (cl**ow**n, cl**ou**d, c**oi**ns, t**oy**s, cr**ew**)

• Lea el poema en la página 81. Hablen sobre la forma en que el corredor se mueve.

• Lea de nuevo el poema. Pida al niño moverse igual que el corredor mientras usted lee.

• Busquen palabras en el poema con vocales controladas por la **r,** vocales dígrafas, y diptongos.

PROJECT

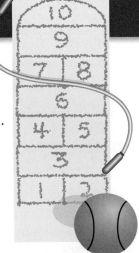

With your child, make a list of sidewalk games or sports, such as hopscotch, hoops, jump rope, and marbles. Circle any vowel combinations in the words on your list. Then play one of the games with your child.

PROYECTO

Hagan una lista de juegos o deportes que se pueden jugar en la acera como por ejemplo: canicas, rayuela, saltar la cuerda. Encierren en un círculo cualquier combinación de vocales en las palabras en su lista. Después jueguen uno de los juegos.

Visit us at **www.sadlierphonicsonline.com**

Name _____

Word Strategy You can use a syllable you know to help you read an unknown word.

car   **car**bon   **car**go   **car**pet   **car**ton

Say the syllable at the beginning of each row. **Circle** the words that begin with the same syllable.

1.	**gar**	garden	gerbil	garbage	gurgle
2.	**per**	party	person	perfect	porridge
3.	**cir**	circle	carton	corner	circus
4.	**for**	furry	faraway	forget	forbid
5.	**tur**	turtle	turkey	tornado	target
6.	**mar**	merchant	market	marbles	murmur
7.	**cur**	corner	cursive	carpet	current

Write a word from the box to complete each sentence. Use the syllable clues to help you.

order	party	perfect	
tortoise	circle	person	cartoon

per   **8.** "Statues" is a _____ lawn game.

par   **9.** It's a good game for a _____.

or   **10.** You don't need to _____ special equipment.

per   **11.** Ask one _____ to be the statue maker.

cir   **12.** He or she will swing you around in a _____ and tell you what to be.

car   **13.** Perhaps you can be a _____ or story character.

tor   **14.** Do you think you'd make a good _____ or hare?

Lesson 45 • Syllables in Words with **r**-Controlled Vowels   **87**

Syllables

Draw a line from a syllable in the first column to a syllable in the second column to make a word. **Write** the word.

1.

air	ful	_____
rare	cut	_____
cheer	port	_____
hair	ly	_____

2.

arm	chair	_____
rein	ware	_____
a	pare	_____
pre	deer	_____

3.

stair	y	_____
near	ring	_____
dair	by	_____
ear	way	_____

4.

re	clear	_____
be	mare	_____
un	ware	_____
night	pair	_____

Work Together Work with a partner. **Write** the two-syllable word from above that fits each clue.

5. It begins with **cheer.**
It's another word for **happy.**

The word is _____.

6. It begins with **near.**
It means "close at hand."

The word is _____.

7. It begins with **dair.**
It's where milk and cream are kept.

The word is _____.

8. It ends with **clear.**
It describes bad directions.

The word is _____.

9. It ends with **ware.**
It means "watch out."

The word is _____.

10. It ends with **pair.**
It's another word for **fix.**

The word is _____.

11. It ends with **chair.**
It's a comfortable seat.

The word is _____.

12. It ends with **deer.**
It's an Arctic animal.

The word is _____.

PHONICS ALIVE AT HOME With your child, write a riddle for each of the following words: **airport, earring, prepare, rarely.**

Name _____

Spell, Write, and Tell **Read** the phrases in the box. **Say** and **spell** each word in **bold** print. **Repeat** the word. **Sort** the words according to sound and spelling.

cheer for the team

throw a **curve** ball

earn points

play **fair**

hear the crowd yell

on your **mark**

a **perfect** game

keep **score**

share the credit

a popular **sport**

the **third** strike

wear a uniform

hard **work**

run nine **yards**

ar in star

_____

_____

or in torch

_____

_____

or in world

or _____

er _____

ir _____

ur _____

ear _____

air in chair

air _____

are _____

ear _____

ear in spear

ear _____

eer _____

Spelling and Writing

Spell, Write, and Tell

Be a sportswriter. **Write** an article about one of your favorite games or events. Begin with a lead sentence that tells **who, what, when,** and **where.** Use one or more of the words in the box in your article.

cheer	curve	earn	fair	hear	mark	perfect
score	share	sport	third	wear	work	yards

↑ headline

by ——————————————————— ← byline

90 **Lesson 46** • Connecting Spelling, Writing, and Speaking

PHONICS ALIVE AT HOME

Together, read your child's article. Ask your child to point out the lead sentence.

Name _____

Write a word from the box for each clue. **Read** down to find the answer to the question.

chair	door	early	girl	herd	horse	near
nurse	pear	square	star	steer	word	worm

1. not a doctor, but a ___   __ __ __ __ __

2. apple, peach, or ___   __ __ __

3. ride a ___ or pony   __ __ __ __ __

4. an antler of a ___   __ __ __ __

5. ___ a bike or car   __ __ __ __

6. not a circle, but a ___   __ __ __ __ __ __

7. an ___ bird   __ __ __ __ __

8. not far, but ___   __ __ __ __

9. a ___ in a puzzle   __ __ __ __ __

10. not a boy, but a ___   __ __ __ __

11. throne, bench, or ___   __ __ __ __ __

12. crawl like a ___   __ __ __ __

13. a ___ of cows   __ __ __ __

14. a ___ athlete   __ __ __ __

What is the theme of this unit?

_____

Check-Up **Say** the name of the picture. **Circle** and **write** the word that names each one.

1. gear girl guard _____	**2.** car curl corn _____	**3.** per purr pear _____
4. world word worn _____	**5.** born barn burn _____	**6.** deer door dare _____
7. porch pearl perch _____	**8.** spare spear spur _____	**9.** chair cheer chore _____

Check-Up **Fill in** the circle next to the word that fits each clue.

10. It's an animal with horns, or what you do in a bike rodeo.
⭘ store ⭘ steer ⭘ stare

11. It's a carnival, or a word that describes someone who is a good sport.
⭘ fair ⭘ fear ⭘ fern

12. It's a kind of baseball pitch, or the shape of the letter **S.**
⭘ car ⭘ curve ⭘ care

13. It's a park in the center of town, or the shape of a checkerboard.
⭘ squirt ⭘ squirrel ⭘ square

14. It's a very good player, or what you see in the night sky.
⭘ star ⭘ stair ⭘ stir

15. It's an animal you can ride, or something a gymnast jumps over.
⭘ hairs ⭘ horse ⭘ hers

PHONICS ALIVE AT HOME Review this Check-Up with your child.

Name _____

Here's a Hint! A **vowel digraph** is two letters together that stand for one vowel sound. The vowel sound can be long or short, or the vowel digraph can have a sound of its own.

Listen for the different sounds of the vowel digraph **ea.**

h**ea**d   s**ea**t

Say the words in the box. **Write** the short **e** words under the head.
Write the long **e** words under the seat.

bread	each	eat	health	leaf
meals	spread	sweat	team	thread

1. Short **e**

_____

_____

_____

_____

_____

2. Long **e**

_____

_____

_____

_____

_____

Write a word from above to complete each sentence.

3. Good _____ helps you enjoy sports.

4. To keep fit, you have to exercise _____ day.

5. It's good to work up a _____.

6. It's also important to _____ well.

7. You should eat balanced _____.

8. That means meat, fruits, vegetables, milk, and _____.

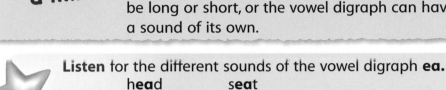

Vowel Digraphs

Listen for the different sounds of the vowel digraph **ei.**

rein   ceiling

Say the words in the box. **Write** the long **a** words under the rein. **Write** the long **e** words under the ceiling.

eight	either	freight	neigh	neighbor	neither
receive	reindeer	seize	sleigh	veil	weight

1.

Long **a**

_____ _____

_____ _____

_____ _____

_____ _____

2.

Long **e**

_____

_____

_____

_____

Circle each word with the vowel digraph **ei. Write yes** or **no** to answer the question.

3. Is a ceiling at the bottom of a room? _____

4. Can a team of reindeer or dogs pull a sleigh? _____

5. Can a girl play a game with a neighbor? _____

6. Does either a cat or dog neigh? _____

7. Can lifting weights help you stay in shape? _____

8. Do you use reins to drive a freight train? _____

9. Can a bride wear a veil with her dress? _____

Write on Track

Rewrite one "yes" question so that the answer is **no.**
Rewrite one "no" question so that the answer is **yes.**

PHONICS
ALIVE AT HOME

With your child, take turns asking and answering the questions at the bottom of the page.

Name _____

Listen for the different sounds of the vowel digraph **oo**.
h**oo**k   b**oo**t
Write the word that fits each clue.

book	brook	foot	good
hook	stood	woods	wool

1. You use this to catch fish. _____

2. This is a small stream. _____

3. This is the opposite of **bad.** _____

4. This is winter material. _____

5. This is a place to set up camp. _____

6. You can stand on this. _____

7. This is a form of the word **stand.** _____

8. You read this. _____

boot	food	loose	noon
pool	smooth	soon	too

9. This is another word for **also.** _____

10. You wear this on your foot. _____

11. This is the opposite of **rough.** _____

12. This is the opposite of **tight.** _____

13. This is a place to go swimming. _____

14. This means "in a short time." _____

15. This is a time of day. _____

16. You eat this. _____

Vowel Digraphs

 The vowel digraphs **au, aw,** and **al** have the same vowel sound.   **lau**nch   str**aw**   b**all**
Say the name of the picture. **Write** the word that names each one.

August	ball	chalk	crawl	faucet	hawk
launch	salt	straw	vault	wall	yawn

1. _____

2. _____

3. _____

4. _____

5. _____

6. _____

7. _____

8. _____

9. _____

10. _____

11. _____

12. _____

Circle and **write** the word that completes each sentence.

13. Baseball usually makes me _____.   yawn   dawn

14. But the last game in _____ was really exciting.   awning   August

15. The first two batters _____.   vault   walked

16. The next batter watched the ball like a _____.   hawk   haul

17. Then he hit it toward the left _____.   wall   call

18. I _____ it sail into the stands.   raw   saw

19. Guess who caught the _____!   ball   straw

Lesson 49 • Recognizing and Writing Vowel Digraphs **au, aw, al**

PHONICS ALIVE AT HOME   Ask your child to use each answer choice that is not circled in items 13–19 in a sentence.

Name _____

 Word Strategy You can use a syllable you know to help you read an unknown word.

head **read**y in**stead**

Write the one-syllable word that you can use to help you read each two-syllable word.

1.	hawk head pea weigh

ready _____

neighbor _____

awkward _____

eager _____

2.	call freight too bread

instead _____

lightweight _____

igloo _____

softball _____

3.	all beak book vein

rookie _____

also _____

weaken _____

reindeer _____

4.	ball sweat seal soon

oatmeal _____

cartoon _____

sweater _____

snowfall _____

 Work Together Write a two-syllable word from above to answer each question. **Compare** answers with a partner.

5. What word with the digraph **ei** names an Arctic animal? _____

6. What word with the digraph **ea** names something you wear? _____

7. What word with the digraph **aw** is the opposite of **graceful?** _____

8. What word with the digraph **oo** is a first-year player? _____

9. What word with the digraph **ea** names a cereal? _____

10. What word with the digraph **oo** is a funny drawing? _____

11. What word with the digraph **al** names a summer sport? _____

Word Strategy

You can use a syllable you know to help you read an unknown word.

head a**head**

Read each riddle. **Look** at the syllables in the words in **bold** print and **write** the two-syllable word that fits the clue.

1. It starts like **around.**
   It ends like **forehead.**
   It means "in front."

   The word is _____.

2. It starts like **seaweed.**
   It ends like **poison.**
   It's a time of the year.

   The word is _____.

3. It starts like **toothbrush.**
   It ends like **weightless.**
   It describes a baby.

   The word is _____.

4. It starts like **mushy.**
   It ends like **classroom.**
   It's also a toadstool.

   The word is _____.

5. It starts like **repeat.**
   It ends like **deceive.**
   It means "to get."

   The word is _____.

6. It starts like **walnut.**
   It ends like **virus.**
   It's an animal with tusks.

   The word is _____.

7. It starts like **footprint.**
   It ends like **baseball.**
   It's a fall sport.

   The word is _____.

8. It starts like **autumn.**
   It ends like **photo.**
   It's another word for **car.**

   The word is _____.

Write on Track

Work with a classmate to write a riddle for a two-syllable word. Challenge a friend to solve it.

PHONICS ALIVE AT HOME Take turns reading and answering the riddles with your child.

Name _____

Spell, Write, and Tell

Read the phrases in the box. **Say** and **spell** each word in **bold** print. **Repeat** the word. **Sort** the words according to sound and spelling.

caught the ball

eager to play

at **either** end

not my **fault**

a **good** game

get **ready**

smooth sailing

be over **soon**

work up a **sweat**

make the **team**

walk to first base

lift **weights**

into the **woods**

makes me **yawn**

ea in **head**	**ea** in **seat**
_____	_____
_____	_____

eigh in **eight**	**ei** in **ceiling**
_____	_____

oo in **hook** or **boot**	**au** in **launch**
_____	au _____
_____	aw _____
_____	al _____
_____	augh _____

Spell, Write, and Tell

Imagine what it's like to be a bat, a ball, or even a bench at a ball game. **Write** a paragraph telling how you feel. Be sure to use the word **I** and one or more of the words in the box. Share your paragraph with the class.

caught	eager	either	fault	good	ready	smooth
soon	sweat	team	walk	weights	woods	yawn

Lesson 51 • Connecting Spelling, Writing, and Speaking

PHONICS ALIVE AT HOME

Ask your child to read his or her paragraph to you and to point out words with vowel combinations.

Name _____

Review

Read the selection about a Chinese game.
Answer the questions.

In China dragons mean good luck. So dragons are part of each New Year's celebration. You can join the fun by playing a game called 1-2-3 Dragon. Here is how to play.

Line up with at least eight other children. Put your hands on the shoulders of the person ahead of you. The very first person becomes the Dragon's Head. The last person becomes the Dragon's Tail.

The Tail starts the game by screaming "1-2-3 Dragon!" Then the Dragon starts to run. The Head leads the way, and the others hold on. The Head tries to seize and tag the Tail without breaking the Dragon.

This is not as easy as it sounds. Holding on makes moving awkward. As the Dragon twists and turns, the line gets crooked. If it falls apart, the Dragon is dead. The Head moves to the end of the line and becomes the Tail. A new Head tries to catch the Dragon's Tail.

1. What is the point of the game 1-2-3 Dragon?

_____

_____

2. What happens when the Dragon "breaks"?

_____

_____

3. How do you think points are scored in this game?

_____

_____

Check-Up Say the word at the beginning of each row.
Circle the words that have the same vowel sound.

1.	**ball**	ahead	also	straw	wool
2.	**head**	weaken	smooth	thread	bread
3.	**hook**	hawk	book	oatmeal	woods
4.	**rein**	sleigh	walrus	freight	either
5.	**launch**	salt	yawn	leaf	mushroom
6.	**seat**	health	weight	seize	season
7.	**boot**	vault	noon	too	chalk
8.	**ceiling**	receive	reins	team	ready

Check-Up **Fill in** the circle next to the word that makes sense in each sentence.

9. It's fun to go skating with your ____.
   ○ neighbors   ○ either   ○ neither

10. Use your ____ and you'll have a good time.
   ○ health   ○ hood   ○ head

11. Make sure your skates are neither ____ nor tight.
   ○ loom   ○ loose   ○ lease

12. Wear a helmet in case you ____.
   ○ fool   ○ crawl   ○ fall

13. ____ wear elbow, knee, and wrist pads.
   ○ Autumn   ○ August   ○ Also

14. Don't worry if your ankles are ____ at first.
   ○ walk   ○ weak   ○ wool

15. Just practice! ____ you'll do fine.
   ○ Soon   ○ Seat   ○ Saw

PHONICS ALIVE AT HOME Review this Check-Up with your child.

Read and Write Ads usually mix fact and opinion. A fact is true. It can be proved. An opinion cannot be proved. **Read** the ad. **Think** about which sentences state facts and which give opinions. **Answer** the questions.

NEW **Zippies Sneakers!**

Finally they're here! They're the latest and greatest! The perfect sneakers! New **Zippies!**

Zippies are the most comfortable sneakers you'll ever wear! They are made of soft, smooth leather. They have special padding in the heels. They have extra space for your toes.

What's more, **Zippies** are the best-looking sneakers in the world! They come in five different styles and colors. Choose from Sparkle Red, Marble Blue, Turtle Green, Torch Yellow, and Pearl White.

And here's another great thing. All this month, you'll receive a free **Zippies** shirt with each pair that you purchase.

So run, don't walk, to your nearest store. Get yourself a pair of **Zippies!**

I. What facts about Zippies sneakers are stated in the ad? List two.

_____

_____

2. What opinions about Zippies sneakers are given in the ad? List two.

_____

_____

Imagine that you have a pair of Zippies. Are they as good as the ad claims? **Write** a letter to the Zippies company. **Tell** why you like or dislike the sneakers and the ad. Use one or more words from the box.

Writer's Tips
- Use the business letter form.
- Introduce yourself and tell why you are writing the letter.
- Give facts and details to support your opinion.
- Be polite.

care	each	neighborhood	return	sports	wear
comfortable	foot	perfect	softball	too	worst

heading ⟶ _____

_____

_____

Customer Service
Zippies Sneakers ⟵ inside address
400 High Street
Shoetown, USA 10001

Dear Sir or Madam, ⟵ greeting   body

_____

_____

_____

_____

_____

_____

closing ⟶ _____

signature ⟶ _____

104

Lesson 53 • Writing **r**-Controlled Vowels and
Vowel Digraphs in Context
Comprehension: Distinguishing Fact from Opinion

PHONICS ALIVE AT HOME

Ask your child to read his or her letter to you. Together, write a letter from Zippies in response.

Name _____

 Here's a Hint! A **diphthong** is two letters blended together that stand for one vowel sound.

 The diphthongs **ow** and **ou** have the same vowel sound.

cl**ow**n   cl**ou**d

Say the name of the picture. **Write** the word that names each one.

1.	clown claw clod _____	2.	cow loud cloud _____	3.	howl how house _____
4.	all owl out _____	5.	drown round brown _____	6.	pouch pound proud _____
7.	pow plow pout _____	8.	count couch crowd _____	9.	crown crawl frown _____

 Write a word from the box to complete each sentence.

around	clowns	down	ground	how

10. Years ago people learned _____ to ski across deep snow.

11. Now skiing is a popular sport _____ the world.

12. Alpine skiers zoom _____ steep hills.

13. Cross-country skiers often glide over flat _____.

14. Freestyle skiers called "hotdoggers" act like _____.

Diphthongs

Here's a Hint! Sometimes the letters **ou** stand for other vowel sounds.

cougar   c**ou**ntry

Read each phrase. **Circle** the word with the letters **ou**.
Write the word under the correct heading.

	ou in **cougar**	**ou** in **country**
1. good to hear from you	_____	_____
2. a couple of bicycle tires	_____	_____
3. score a touchdown	_____	_____
4. sip a bowl of soup	_____	_____
5. a group of friends	_____	_____
6. several young athletes	_____	_____
7. save coupons	_____	_____
8. play a double header	_____	_____
9. enough seats for all	_____	_____
10. follow a routine	_____	_____
11. sail the rough seas	_____	_____
12. a troupe of acrobats	_____	_____
13. a first cousin	_____	_____

Work Together   **Write** a sentence using two or more words with **ou**. **Read** your sentence to a partner.

_____

_____

Lesson 54 • Recognizing the Sounds of **ou**

PHONICS ALIVE AT HOME   Ask your child to read the words in one list to you. Read the words in the other list to your child.

The diphthongs **oi** in **coins** and **oy** in **toys** have the same vowel sound. The diphthong **ew** has the vowel sound in **screw**.   c**oi**ns   t**oy**s   scr**ew**
Say the words in the box. **Sort** the words according to their vowel sound.
Write each word under the correct heading.

annoy	boil	drew	flew	join	joy
knew	loyal	new	noise	spoil	toys

1.

oi in coins

_____ _____

_____ _____

_____ _____

_____ _____

2.

ew in screw

_____

_____

_____

_____

   Use each pair of words to **write** a sentence.

3. noise, annoys _____

_____

4. join, crew _____

_____

5. boy, enjoys _____

_____

6. few, blew _____

_____

Syllables

Word Strategy You can use a syllable you know to help you read an unknown word.   pow **pow**er   joy en**joy**

Draw a line from a syllable in the first column to a syllable in the second column to make a word. **Write** the word.

1.
pow   how   _____
eye   er   _____
some   down   _____
touch   brow   _____

2.
out   round   _____
play   doors   _____
a   ground _____
cloud   y   _____

3.
spoil   ing   _____
en   y   _____
nois   al   _____
loy   joy   _____

4.
few   new   _____
re   few   _____
neph   er   _____
cur   ew   _____

Complete each line of the poem by **writing** a two-syllable word from above. Use the syllable clues to help you.

Let's Hear It for Fans!

loy   Our team has very _____ fans.

nois   They're really _____ in the stands.

cloud   And even on a _____ day,

out   They'll come _____ to watch us play.

round   The fans _____ us cheer out loud,

new   _____ our spirits, make us proud.

pow   It's their cheers that give us _____.

Let's name our fans "Fans of the Hour."

PHONICS ALIVE AT HOME Ask your child to explain how he or she completed the poem. Then take turns reading pairs of lines.

Name _____

Spell, Write, and Tell

Read the phrases in the box. Say and spell each word in **bold** print. Repeat the word. Sort the words according to sound and spelling.

act like **clowns**

collect **coins**

join the **crew**

a large **crowd**

enjoy the game

make **fewer** moves

flew a kite

in the **house**

a **loyal** teammate

too much **noise**

the third **out**

make us **proud**

spoil the fun

threw the ball

ou in **cloud**

ow _____

_____

ou _____

_____

_____

oy in **toys**

oi _____

_____

_____

oy _____

_____

ew in **screw**

_____

_____

_____

_____

Cheer on your favorite team! First use a word from the box to complete the cheer. **Write** two cheers of your own, using one or more of the words.

clowns	coins	crew	crowd	enjoy	fewer	flew
house	loyal	noise	out	proud	spoil	threw

Stamp your feet!
Cheer and shout!
Watch our pitchers

strike them _____!

_____

_____

_____

_____

_____

_____

_____

_____

_____

_____

_____

_____

110 Lesson 57 • Connecting Spelling, Writing, and Speaking

 Ask your child to lead you in a cheer. Then write a cheer together. Use one or more of the words in the box.

Name _____

Review

Complete the puzzle. **Write** a word from the box for each clue.

annoy	cloudy	crew	crowd	down	onjoy	cyobrow	fcwcr

flew	join	loyal	noise	outdoors	outs	owl

ACROSS ➡

1. less than a few
3. covered with clouds
4. be happy with
7. the opposite of **indoors**
8. pester
10. a large group of people
12. more than one out
13. a wise bird

DOWN ⬇

1. a form of the word **fly**
2. hair above the eye
5. put together
6. faithful
9. another word for **sound**
10. the sailors on a ship
11. the opposite of **up**

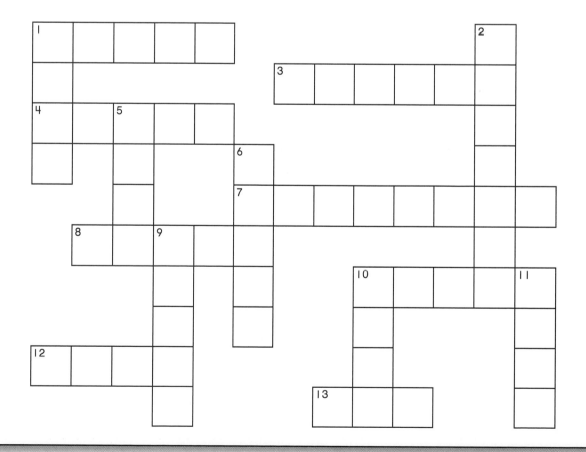

 Check-Up Say the word at the beginning of each row.
Circle the words that have the same vowel sound.

1.	**clown**	clean	owl	foul	draw
2.	**toys**	coins	boy	group	couch
3.	**screw**	few	screen	new	now
4.	**join**	bone	boil	jail	joy
5.	**cloud**	fold	pouch	ground	claw
6.	**threw**	blew	three	thaw	drew
7.	**crowd**	crawl	crown	news	plow
8.	**spoil**	noise	split	coil	trail

Check-Up Fill in the circle next to the word that makes sense in each sentence.

9. When the wind blows hard, surfers go ＿＿ to the beach.
   ○ down   ○ dawn   ○ dew

10. These are people who ＿＿ riding the waves.
   ○ joy   ○ enjoy   ○ annoy

11. The ＿＿ roar of the ocean is music to their ears.
   ○ lead   ○ loud   ○ load

12. Some surf with speed and with ＿＿ .
   ○ powder   ○ tower   ○ power

13. A ＿＿ will even beat the wind.
   ○ flew   ○ few   ○ foul

14. They all know that surfboards and sailboards are not ＿＿ .
   ○ toys   ○ toes   ○ tows

15. Only the best swimmers ＿＿ in on this sport.
   ○ spoil   ○ coin   ○ join

PHONICS ALIVE AT HOME Review this Check-Up with your child.

Name_____

Here's a Hint! Some word families are spelled in unusual ways. Word families with these phonograms have the long **a**, long **i**, long **e**, or long **u** sounds.

Long **a**	rein	Long **i**	fight	Long **e**	field	Long **u**	moon
	weight		high		chief		room
	straight						

For each word, **write** the phonogram and the long vowel sound it makes.

		Phonogram	**Vowel Sound**
1.	soon	_____	_____
2.	shield	_____	_____
3.	thigh	_____	_____
4.	brief	_____	_____
5.	might	_____	_____
6.	thief	_____	_____
7.	spoon	_____	_____
8.	broom	_____	_____
9.	yield	_____	_____
10.	eight	_____	_____
11.	rein	_____	_____
12.	groom	_____	_____
13.	vein	_____	_____
14.	freight	_____	_____
15.	tight	_____	_____
16.	sigh	_____	_____

Complex Word Families

Here's a Hint! Word families with these phonograms have the sounds of the **oi, ou,** and **ow** diphthongs.

join	pout
loud	mouse
round	town

⭐ **Read** each word. **Underline** the phonogram. **Write** another word with the same phonogram.

1. join _____
2. loud _____
3. ground _____
4. shout _____
5. house _____
6. town _____

⭐ **Work Together** Choose five words from above and use each one in a sentence. **Share** your sentences with a partner.

7. _____
_____

8. _____
_____

9. _____
_____

10. _____
_____

11. _____
_____

114 **Lesson 59** • Recognizing and Writing Complex Word Families

Point to a word and ask your child to name other words he or she knows that are spelled with the same phonogram.

Name _____

Here's a Hint! Word families with these phonograms have the sounds of the **au, aw, oo,** and **ea** digraphs.

au, aw thought   **oo** took   **ea** head
         caught
         lawn
         talk

Complete the puzzle. **Write** a word from the box for each clue. When you've finished the puzzle, **color** the boxes containing the letters in the phonograms.

book	bread	chalk	fought	hook	walk
bought	caught	dawn	head	taught	yawn

ACROSS ➡

2. you can eat this
7. part of your body
8. when you argued with someone
9. you do this when you're tired
10. to move one step at a time
11. something to hang a coat on

DOWN ⬇

1. captured
2. paid for at a store
3. early morning
4. educated you about something
5. you can write with this
6. you can read this

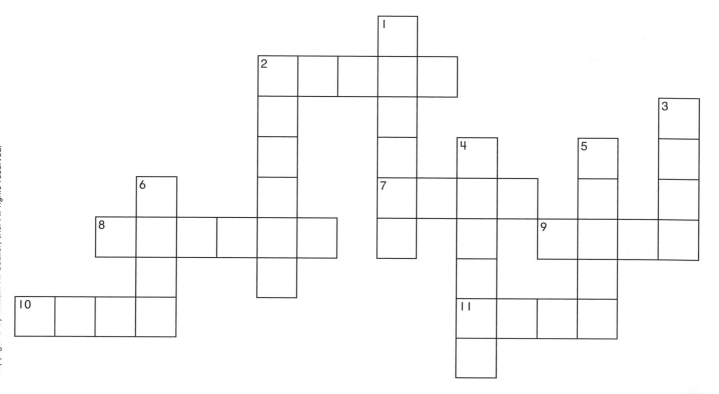

Read each word. **Write** a word with the same phonogram.

1. yield _____	2. freight _____	3. stood _____
4. coin _____	5. pound _____	6. yawn _____
7. grief _____	8. rein _____	9. caught _____
10. moon _____	11. bought _____	12. talk _____
13. brown _____	14. shout _____	15. bread _____
16. room _____	17. light _____	18. house _____
19. cloud _____	20. look _____	21. sprout _____

PHONICS ALIVE AT HOME Ask your child to read each word he or she wrote.

Name _____

Read and Write **Read** the article about a famous race. Pay attention to details. **Answer** the questions.

Race Across Alaska

It's a race like no other. It's famous around the world. And it's probably the toughest race there is. It's called the Iditarod, and it's held every year in Alaska.

In this amazing race, teams of dogs pull sleds across more than 1,000 miles of ice, deep snow, and rough woods. Each team has between 12 and 18 dogs. Each sled has a driver, called a "musher."

About 75 teams begin the race, which takes from two to three weeks. But not all reach the finish line. The frozen ground is rough, uneven, and often steep. Temperatures go down far below zero. The howling wind whips snow around so that drivers and dogs cannot see.

Still, mushers and dogs come back year after year because they enjoy the challenge. "If you finish at all," says one racer, "you feel like you've won."

1. How many dogs are on each sled team?

_____

_____

2. Give two reasons why many teams do not reach the finish line.

_____

_____

Lesson 61 • Applying Skills in Context
Comprehension: Recalling Details

Phonics and Writing

Would you like to race in the Iditarod? Why or why not? **Write** a paragraph in which you tell your feelings about taking part in this challenging event. Use one or more words from the box.

Writer's Tips

- Begin with a topic sentence that tells whether or not you would like to take part in the race.
- Give at least two reasons why you feel the way you do. Use details from the article to help explain your feelings.

| before | down | few | join | rough | stood |
| breath | enjoy | harder | powerful | scare | young |

Lesson 61 • Writing Diphthongs and Complex Word Families in Context
Comprehension: Recalling Details

PHONICS ALIVE AT HOME

Ask your child to read his or her paragraph to you. Discuss your feelings about the Iditarod with your child.

Name _____

READ

Let's **read** and **talk** about jumping rope.

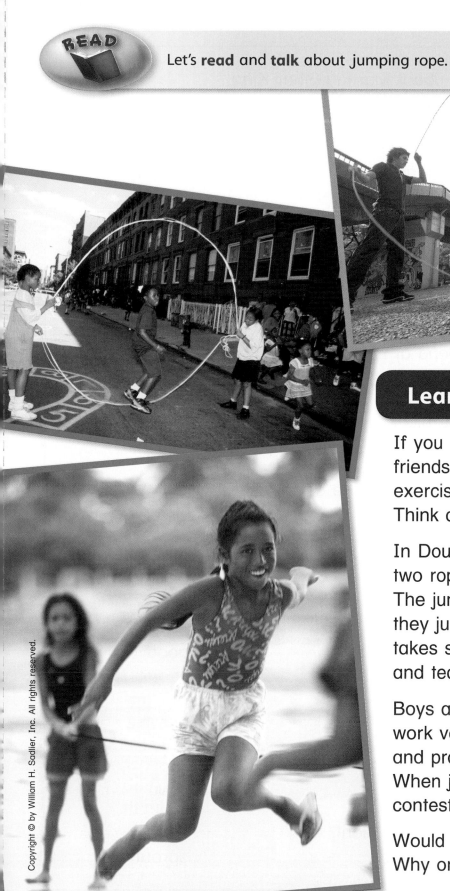

Learn About Jumping Rope

If you have ever jumped rope with your friends, you know jumping rope is good exercise and fun, too. But is it a sport? Think about Double Dutch jump teams.

In Double Dutch, pairs of twirlers turn two ropes at once in opposite directions. The jumpers either dance or tumble as they jump. Performing on a jump team takes strength, energy, coordination, and teamwork.

Boys and girls who join jump teams all work very hard. They carefully prepare and practice new tricks with their team. When jumpers are ready, they enter contests and appear in shows.

Would you call jumping rope a sport? Why or why not?

Lesson 62 • r-Controlled Vowels, Vowel Digraphs, Diphthongs, and Complex Word Families in Context
Comprehension: Making Judgments
Developing Fluency

 **Assessment**

1. The teacher gave a ____ talk about Martin Luther King.
   ○ weight   ○ brief   ○ field

2. My two sisters ____ over the same red sweater.
   ○ bought   ○ taught   ○ fought

3. I grabbed my bike and pedaled ____ home.
   ○ light   ○ freight   ○ straight

4. Our class talked about ____ when the hamster died.
   ○ grief   ○ thief   ○ sleigh

5. I ____ a giant fish from the pond at the park.
   ○ thought   ○ caught   ○ crook

6. I took a short ____ around the block.
   ○ walk   ○ wood   ○ house

7. It was cold, but we all went for a long ride on the ____.
   ○ sight   ○ spread   ○ sleigh

8. The man ____ at the very top of the stairs.
   ○ scout   ○ stood   ○ soon

9. I like peanut butter on my ____.
   ○ bread   ○ bright   ○ good

10. My new ____ has a hole in the sleeve.
    ○ block   ○ blouse   ○ blown

11. I couldn't help but ____ as I listened to the speech.
    ○ yawn   ○ yield   ○ fawn

12. I saw a little green ____ on my bean plant.
    ○ shout   ○ sound   ○ sprout

PHONICS **ALIVE AT HOME** With your child, make up sentences that use some of the words on the page.

Name _____

An Amazing Birthday Game

Let me introduce myself. My name is Jack, and my sister's name is Mary. Our father is the gardener for the Duke and Duchess of Beltrain. I became friendly with their son, Harry. He invited Mary and me to his tenth birthday party. I thought the party would be boring, but I had quite an adventure.

Fold

Help Jack and Harry find their way out of the maze. Then write your own ending for the story.

DIRECTIONS: Cut and fold the book.

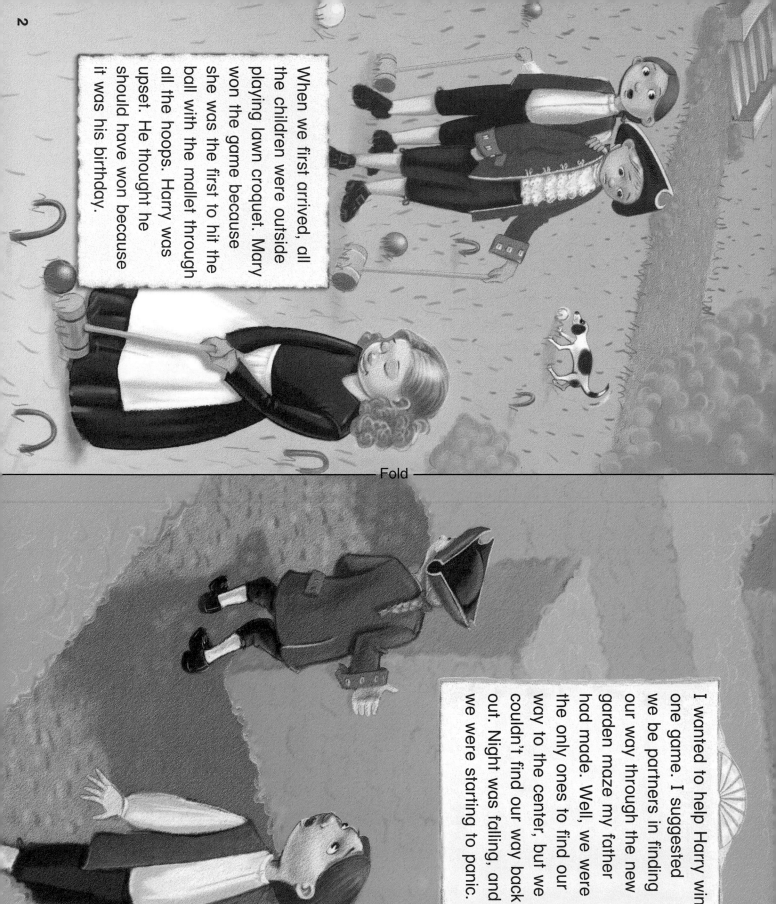

2

When we first arrived, all the children were outside playing lawn croquet. Mary won the game because she was the first to hit the ball with the mallet through all the hoops. Harry was upset. He thought he should have won because it was his birthday.

3

I wanted to help Harry win one game. I suggested we be partners in finding our way through the new garden maze my father had made. Well, we were the only ones to find our way to the center, but we couldn't find our way back out. Night was falling, and we were starting to panic.

I Made a Mechanical Dragon

I made a mechanical dragon
Of bottle tops, hinges, and strings,
Of thrown-away clocks and unmendable socks,
Of hangers and worn innersprings.
I built it of cardboard and plastic,
Of doorknobs and cables and corks,
Of spools and balloons and unusable spoons,
And rusty old hinges and forks.

It's quite an unusual dragon
It rolls on irregular wheels,
It clatters and creaks and it rattles and squeaks,
And when it tips over, it squeals.
I've tried to control its maneuvers,
It fails to obey my commands,
It bumps into walls till it totters and falls—
I made it myself with my hands!

Jack Prelutsky

Critical Thinking What materials would you use to make a mechanical dragon? What would you like to invent? How would you go about it?

Name _____

Dear Family,

As your child progresses through this unit about inventions, she or he will learn about contractions and word endings. Share these definitions:

> **contraction:** two words written as one with one or more letters left out (**didn't = did not; she'll = she will**)
>
> **plural:** word that means more than one (**pencils, boxes, leaves**)
>
> **possessive:** word that shows something belongs to someone (**the girl's bike; ten girls' bikes**)
>
> **word endings s, es, ing, and ed:** endings that can be added to a word to make new words (**paints, fixes, running, smiled**)

- Read the poem on the reverse side. Invite your child to clap out the rhythm as you read.

- Take turns finding rhyming words in the poem, such as **strings** and **springs.** Also look for contractions, plurals, and words that end in **s** or **ed.**

Apreciada Familia,

A medida que los niños progresan en esta unidad acerca de los inventos, aprenderán contracciones y terminaciones. Compartan estas definiciones:

> **contracción:** una palabra formada por la abreviación de dos palabras (**didn't = did not; she'll = she will**)
>
> **plural:** palabras que indican más de uno (**pencils, boxes, leaves**)
>
> **posesivo:** palabras que indican que una cosa pertenece a alguien (**the girl's bike; ten girls' bikes**)
>
> **palabras que terminan en s, es, ing, y ed:** letras que se añaden al final de una palabra para formar una nueva (**paints, fixes, running, smiled**)

- Lea el poema en la página 123. Invite al niño a aplaudir rítmicamente mientras usted lee.

- Túrnense para buscar en el poema palabras que rimen como por ejemplo: **strings** y **springs.** También busquen contracciones, plurales y palabras que terminen en **s** o en **ed.**

PROJECT

Help your child write and illustrate a story about life without paper, pencils, or some other invention. Circle contractions and word endings in the story.

PROYECTO

Ayude al niño a escribir e ilustrar un cuento sobre la vida sin papel, lápices o otro invento. Encierren en un círculo las contracciones y palabras con terminaciones.

Name _____

Here's a Hint! Every **syllable** has a vowel sound. Words can have one or more syllables.

umbr**ella**—**3** vowel sounds—**3** syllables

Empty the junk box. **Say** the name of each thing you find and **listen** for the number of vowel sounds. **Write** each word under the correct heading. **Add** a word of your own to each category.

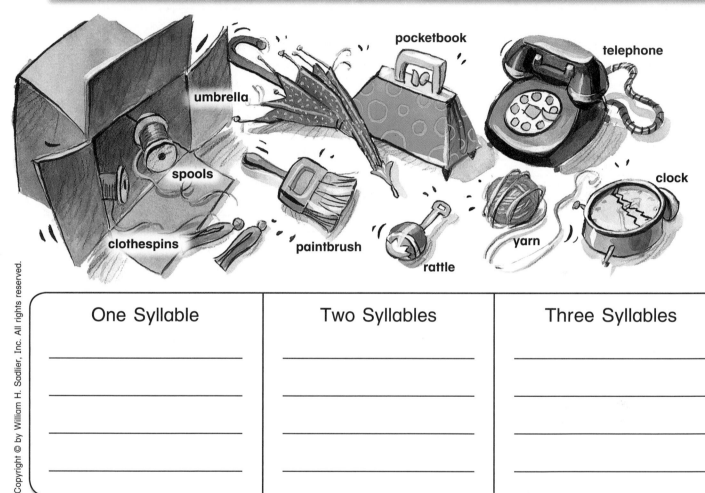

pocketbook

telephone

umbrella

clock

spools

clothespins

paintbrush

rattle

yarn

One Syllable	Two Syllables	Three Syllables
_____	_____	_____
_____	_____	_____
_____	_____	_____
_____	_____	_____

What kind of gadget might you invent from the odds and ends in this junk box? **Write** a sentence or two to describe it. **Circle** each three-syllable word you used.

_____

_____

_____

_____

Syllables

 Word Strategy One way to figure out an unknown word is to divide it into syllables. If a word has two or more consonants between two vowels, you can usually divide the word between the first two consonants.

| **zip-pe**rs | **in-ve**nt | **sur-pri**se |
| VC C V | VC CV | VC C CV |

 Write each word, dividing it into syllables with a hyphen.

1. zippers _____	**2.** surprise _____
3. number _____	**4.** pencil _____
5. invent _____	**6.** problem _____
7. silver _____	**8.** wonder _____
9. hundreds _____	**10.** pilgrim _____
11. attach _____	**12.** fifty _____
13. fabric _____	**14.** tennis _____

Work Together **Write** a word from above to complete each sentence. Take turns **reading** the sentences with a partner.

15. Did you ever _____ why burrs stick to clothes?

16. George de Mestral asked this question about _____ years ago.

17. He noticed that burrs have _____ of tiny hooks.

18. The hooks _____ themselves to thread loops on clothes.

19. Mr. de Mestral set out to _____ a fastener that would work like a burr.

20. His invention has replaced many _____ and buttons.

 PHONICS ALIVE AT HOME Ask your child to use items 1–14 to explain what a VCCV word is.

Name _____

Word Strategy

If a word has one consonant between two vowels, first divide before the consonant. The first vowel sound will usually be long. If you still don't recognize the word, divide after the consonant. The vowel sound will usually be short.

o-ver   mu-sic   pat-ent   clev-er
V CV   V CV   VC V   VC V

Write each word, dividing it into syllables with a hyphen.

1. over _____		**2.** patent _____	
3. figure _____		**4.** cozy _____	
5. never _____		**6.** music _____	
7. clever _____		**8.** frozen _____	
9. level _____		**10.** value _____	

Write a word from above to complete each sentence. **Read** the paragraph about a clever young inventor.

As a young boy, Chester Greenwood liked to skate on a _____ pond near his home. He dressed warmly, but he could _____ keep his ears warm. Chester spent hours trying to _____ out a way to solve his problem. Finally he twisted some wire to fit _____ his head. His grandmother sewed fur on at the ear _____. With his new earmuffs, Chester felt _____ and warm. Chester knew the _____ of his invention and got a _____ for it. What a _____ boy!

Write each word, dividing it into syllables with a hyphen. Use the word strategy for VCV words to help you.

1. dragon _____	**2.** ever _____
3. pilot _____	**4.** river _____
5. finish _____	**6.** famous _____
7. seconds _____	**8.** palace _____
9. travel _____	**10.** lazy _____
11. tiger _____	**12.** magic _____
13. model _____	**14.** robot _____

Work Together Work with a partner. Use each pair of words to **write** a sentence.

15. famous, pilot _____

_____

16. model, robot _____

_____

17. magic, dragon _____

_____

18. ever, travel _____

_____

19. finish, seconds _____

_____

PHONICS ALIVE AT HOME Ask your child to use the words at the top to explain what a VCV word is.

Name _____

Here's a Hint! Some words end in a consonant followed by **le**. The **le** and the consonant before it often form a syllable.

puz-**zle**   ta-**ble**

Say the name of the picture. **Circle** the syllable that completes its name. **Write** the letters to complete the word.

1. zle / kle / cle puz____	**2.** dle / ble / gle ta____	**3.** tle / ple / dle peo____
4. ple / ble / tle tur____	**5.** zle / kle / gle an____	**6.** ble / cle / ple ap____
7. zle / cle / gle cir____	**8.** gle / kle / tle jug____	**9.** ple / dle / tle rat____
10. ble / dle / kle can____	**11.** cle / tle / ble bot____	**12.** gle / zle / ple ea____
13. cle / kle / dle nee____	**14.** ple / tle / gle pur____	**15.** dle / ble / kle thim____

Word Strategy You can use a syllable you know to help you read an unknown word.

ple ap**ple** ma**ple** pur**ple** sam**ple**

Draw a line from a syllable in the first column to a syllable in the second column to make words. **Write** the words.

1.
ap	tle	_____
han	dle	_____
bu	ple	_____
gen	gle	_____

2.
bub	zle	_____
un	fle	_____
siz	cle	_____
ruf	ble	_____

3.
noo	dle	_____
spar	kle	_____
rip	ble	_____
sta	ple	_____

4.
ea	dle	_____
tur	ble	_____
a	tle	_____
sad	gle	_____

Circle and **write** the word that completes each sentence.

5. This is a very _____ invention.   sample   simple

6. It does not have a _____.   handle   cuddle

7. It is round like a _____.   uncle   circle

8. It can be big or _____.   little   able

9. _____ have many uses for it.   Purple   People

10. A _____ has two of them.   bicycle   icicle

11. A _____ has three of them.   twinkle   tricycle

12. Can you solve the _____?   ripple   riddle

Write on Track

Think of some uses for this invention. Work with a classmate to make a list.

PHONICS ALIVE AT HOME Together, make up sentences using the words in the boxes at the top of the page.

Here's a Hint! The vowels **a, i, o, u,** and **e** can stand for the same sound in an unstressed syllable. This sound is called the **schwa** sound.

sal'**a**d   rob'**i**n   lem'**o**n   cir'**cu**s   sev'**e**n

Put the syllables together to **name** each picture. **Circle** the syllable with the **schwa** sound. **Write** the vowel that stands for the sound.

1.	2.	3.	4.
sal'ad ☐	nick'el ☐	pen'cil ☐	lem'on ☐

5.	6.	7.	8.
ketch'up ☐	pret'zel ☐	rib'bon ☐	rob'in ☐

9.	10.	11.	12.
ze'bra ☐	par'rot ☐	sev'en ☐	cir'cus ☐

Write on Track

Work with a classmate to invent and write a recipe for a salad. Circle ingredients with the **schwa** sound.

Word Strategy You can use a syllable in a word you know to help you read an unknown word.
par**rot**   car**rot**

Read each riddle. **Look** at the syllables in the words in **bold** print and **write** the two-syllable word that fits each clue.

1. It starts like **carry**.
   It ends like **parrot**.
   It grows in the ground.

   The word is _____ .

2. It starts like **ago**.
   It ends like **belong**.
   It means "together with."

   The word is _____ .

3. It starts like **robber**.
   It ends like **cabin**.
   It's a spring bird.

   The word is _____ .

4. It starts like **bunny**.
   It ends like **puddle**.
   It's often wrapped up.

   The word is _____ .

5. It starts like **asleep**.
   It ends like **depart**.
   It means "not together."

   The word is _____ .

6. It starts like **metric**.
   It ends like **petal**.
   It's often shiny.

   The word is _____ .

7. It starts like **candy**.
   It ends like **handle**.
   It's something you light.

   The word is _____ .

8. It starts like **circle**.
   It ends like **focus**.
   It's a great show.

   The word is _____ .

9. It starts like **dragging**.
   It ends like **wagon**.
   It's something mechanical.

   The word is _____ .

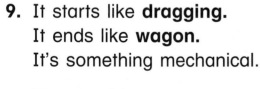

PHONICS ALIVE AT HOME Together, complete this riddle: It starts like **penny**. It ends like **stencil**.

Read the magazine article about a new invention. **Think** about why and how the invention came to be. **Answer** the questions.

Cricket Corral:
A Neat Idea

Picture this scene.

It's 4:00 P.M.—time to feed Myrtle, your pet toad. You open a box of fresh crickets from the pet store. You grab a bunch of the big bugs. They squirm and kick. A few escape into your living room.

Can anything be done about messy mealtimes like these? David Rose and Darby Cunningham thought so. The two inventors recently received a patent for a device they call the "Cricket Corral."

Here's how the invention works. You fill a container with crickets. Then you put on the lid, which has a wide tube sticking out of it. Some of the crickets climb into the tube. When you're ready to feed your pet, just lift out the tube and give it a tap. The crickets fall out. You don't have to touch them. Now that's neat!

1. What made David Rose and Darby Cunningham invent the Cricket Corral?

_____

_____

2. How does the invention work?

_____

_____

Phonics and Writing

Suppose you could interview the inventors of the Cricket Corral. What would you ask? **Write** three or four questions. Use one or more words from the box.

able	apply	device	famous	money	people
admire	create	ever	item	patent	problem

Lesson 72 • Writing Multisyllabic Words, Words Ending in **le**, and Words with Schwa in Context
Comprehension: Summarizing

PHONICS ALIVE AT HOME Ask your child to read his or her interview questions to you. Make up answers to the questions.

Name _____

Here's a Hint! A **contraction** is a short way of writing two words as one. In a contraction, one or more letters are left out. An apostrophe (') shows where the letters were.

doesn't = does n**ot**   we'll = we **will**   she's = she **is** *or* she **ha**s

Write the contraction from the box for each pair of words.

doesn't	haven't	he's	I'd	I'm	I've	let's	she's
they'd	they'll	they're	they've	we'll	won't	you'll	

Contractions with **not**

1. does not	2. have not	3. will not
_____	_____	_____

Contractions with **will**

4. we will	5. they will	6. you will
_____	_____	_____

Contractions with **am, is, are**

7. she is	8. I am	9. they are
_____	_____	_____

Contractions with **have, has**

10. I have	11. they have	12. he has
_____	_____	_____

Contractions with **us, would**

13. let us	14. I would	15. they would
_____	_____	_____

Contracciones

Write the words for each contraction. Use one of the words from the box. **Compare** answers with a partner.

are	has	have	is	not	will	would

1. I'll _____	2. there's _____
3. we'd _____	4. you're _____
5. it's _____	6. can't _____
7. wasn't _____	8. don't _____
9. isn't _____	10. you've _____
11. we've _____	12. shouldn't _____
13. couldn't _____	14. that's _____

What's there to do at home on a rainy day? **Complete** each sentence using a contraction.

15. It rained yesterday, so _____

_____

16. I wanted to have fun, but _____

_____

17. Mom said, "I have a box in the basement that _____

_____

18. That gave me an idea. I built _____

_____

136 Lesson 73 • Recognizing and Writing Contractions

Ask your child to circle the contraction in each sentence and name the words for each contraction.

Name _____

Read the selection about an accidental invention. **Underline** the contractions and **write** the words for the contractions below.

What's shaped like a pig and holds coins? It's a piggy bank, of course. You might think a piggy bank gets its name from its shape, but that's not the case. Here's the story of how little pigs became banks.

In England during the 1400s, jars and pots weren't made from glass or metal. That wouldn't have been practical. Potters used a clay called "pygg" instead. People soon called the jar in which they put their spare change a "pygg jar" or "pygg bank."

As time passed, people didn't remember that pygg was clay. At some point, a potter asked to make a "pygg bank" must have made a bank shaped like a pig. Wasn't that a great mistake! Piggy banks are still popular today.

_____ _____

_____ _____

_____ _____

What do you think would be another good shape for a coin bank? **Write** a sentence or two explaining your choice.

_____

_____

_____

_____

Lesson 74 • Reviewing Contractions   **137**

Check-Up **Write** the contraction for each pair of words.

1. is not _____		**2.** let us _____	
3. she is _____		**4.** do not _____	
5. you will _____		**6.** they are _____	
7. we have _____		**8.** it has _____	
9. I would _____		**10.** there is _____	

Check-Up **Write** the words for each contraction.

11. haven't _____	**12.** doesn't _____
13. they'd _____	**14.** you've _____
15. couldn't _____	**16.** they'll _____
17. that's _____	**18.** won't _____

Check-Up **Circle** the contraction in each sentence. **Write** the words for the contraction.

19. "I've got a problem," said Julia. _____

20. "What's wrong?" asked her friend Kim. _____

21. "I'm always losing my pencils," Julia replied. _____

22. "They're never where I leave them." _____

23. "Why don't we work together?" asked Kim. _____

24. "We'll invent something to help you." _____

PHONICS ALIVE AT HOME Review this Check-Up with your child.

Name _____

Here's a Hint! An apostrophe and an **s** (**'s**) can be added to the end of a word to show ownership.

the tools that belong to **Maria** = **Maria's** tools
the idea of one **person** = one **person's** idea

Rewrite each phrase. **Add 's** to the word in **bold** print to show who owns something.

1. the cat that belongs to **Michael** _____

2. the wagon of **Anita** _____

3. the collar on my **dog** _____

4. the opinion of an **expert** _____

5. the hard drive of the **computer** _____

Work Together **Circle** the phrases that show ownership. Use each circled phrase in a sentence. **Share** your sentences with a partner.

Beth's invention	the dog's toy	Jed's gadget
green leaves	Mom's keys	hearing aids

6. _____

_____

7. _____

_____

8. _____

_____

9. _____

Possessives

Here's a Hint! An apostrophe (') can be added after the final **s** of a plural word to show ownership.

the tools that belong to the **students** = the **students'** tools
the ideas of the **inventors** = the **inventors'** ideas

Rewrite each phrase. **Add** an apostrophe (') to the plural word in **bold** print to show who owns something.

1. the books that belong to my **sisters** _____

2. the inventions of the **scientists** _____

3. the branches of the **trees** _____

4. the feathers on the **birds** _____

5. the rackets that belong to the **players** _____

6. the shoes of the **runners** _____

7. the voices of the **teachers** _____

8. the games that belong to my **brothers** _____

Circle the word that completes each sentence. Choose the word with **s'** when you want to show ownership.

9. My friends and I are starting a ____ club. kids   kids'

10. It's for ____ who like to invent things. kids   kids'

11. The first two ____ will take place at my house. meetings   meetings'

12. Then we'll take turns meeting at other ____ houses. members   members'

13. We've already put together a list of ____. tools   tools'

14. We'll gather the tools and other ____. materials   materials'

15. Then we'll get started on a variety of ____. projects   projects'

16. Don't worry! We'll work under our ____ supervision. parents   parents'

---

144 Lesson 79 • Recognizing and Writing Plural Possessives

PHONICS ALIVE AT HOME Together, replace the plural words in items 1–8 to change ownership, for example, **my friends' books.**

Read the stories of two interesting inventions. **Add s, es, 's,** or **s'** to each root word and **write** a word to complete each sentence. Remember to make spelling changes.

The Lock and the Key

Can you imagine carrying around _____ that
(key)

are over a foot long? That's what you would have done if

you were a wealthy Egyptian 4,000 _____ ago.
(year)

The _____ invented wooden locks with gigantic
(Egyptian)

keys to keep out _____. The Greeks borrowed
(thief)

the _____ idea and passed it on to the Romans.
(Egyptian)

The Ice Cream Cone

It happened in 1904 at the _____ Fair in
(World)

St. Louis. Ernest Hamwi was selling _____ next
(waffle)

to an ice cream vendor. The ice cream vendor ran out of

_____. Mr. Hamwi quickly rolled a waffle into a
(dish)

cone to hold a scoop of his _____ ice cream.
(neighbor)

That day Mr. Hamwi earned the _____ of
(thank)

_____ and friends from all over the world.
(family)

 **Assessment**

 Check-Up **Write** the plural of each root word. Remember to make spelling changes.

1. buddy _____		**2.** wolf _____	
3. key _____		**4.** bus _____	
5. peach _____		**6.** day _____	
7. party _____		**8.** dish _____	
9. life _____		**10.** box _____	

Check-Up **Write** the root word.

11. shelves _____	**12.** foxes _____
13. boys _____	**14.** stories _____
15. bunnies _____	**16.** lunches _____
17. loaves _____	**18.** ponies _____

Check-Up **Rewrite** each phrase. Use **'s** or an apostrophe (') to show ownership.

19. the cows that belong to the farmer _____

20. the windows of the houses _____

21. the dog that belongs to Jamal _____

22. the tails on the bunnies _____

23. the panda that lives at the zoo _____

24. the fins of the sharks _____

146 Lesson 80 • Assessing Plurals and Possessives

PHONICS ALIVE AT HOME Review this Check-Up with your child.

Name _____

Here's a Hint! When a root word ends in **y** after a consonant, change the **y** to **i** before adding **es** or **ed.** When the **y** follows a vowel, just add **s** or **ed.**

ca**rry** + es = ca**rries**   ca**rry** + **ed** = ca**rried**
pl**ay** + s = pl**ays**   pl**ay** + **ed** = pl**ayed**

Add ing and **ed** to each root word. **Write** the new words.

	s or **es**	**ed**
1. carry	_____	_____
2. annoy	_____	_____
3. try	_____	_____
4. worry	_____	_____
5. stay	_____	_____

Read the first sentence in each pair. Complete the second sentence so that it tells about the past. Use a form of the word in **bold** print.

6. Nikki **studies** near an electric lamp.

Nikki's great-grandmother _____ by candlelight.

7. Jenny **plays** the electric guitar.

Jenny's great-grandfather _____ the banjo.

8. Jesse **obeys** the stoplight and crosses at the green.

Jesse's great-grandfather _____ a crossing guard.

9. Aaron **dries** the clothes in a clothes dryer.

Aaron's great-grandmother _____ the clothes on a bush.

Write on Track

Write a pair of sentences comparing the way you do something today with the way a great-grandparent did years ago.

When a root word ends in **e**, drop the final **e** before adding **ing** or **ed**.
sav**e** + **ing** = sav**ing**   sav**e** + **ed** = sav**ed**

⭐ **Drop** the final **e** and **add ing** and **ed** to each root word. **Write** the new words.

		ing	**ed**
1.	save	_____	_____
2.	wipe	_____	_____
3.	hope	_____	_____
4.	exercise	_____	_____
5.	paste	_____	_____
6.	sneeze	_____	_____

Write the root word.

7. waving _____	8. practiced _____
9. cared _____	10. tracing _____
11. erasing _____	12. joked _____

Add ing or **ed** to each word in **bold** print so that the sentence makes sense. **Write** the new word.

13. In 1760 Joseph Merlin **create** a pair of wheeled shoes. _____

14. When he rolled into a party, he **startle** the other guests. _____

15. Unable to stop or steer, he **skate** right into a mirror. _____

16. That might have ended the story of roller **skate**. _____

17. But another inventor found a way of **improve** the skates. _____

 PHONICS ALIVE AT HOME Ask your child to read the corrected sentences to you.

Name _____

Here's a Hint! When a short vowel word ends in a single consonant, double the final consonant before adding **ing** or **ed**.
ski**p** + **ing** = ski**pping**   ski**p** + **ed** = ski**pped**

Double the final consonant and **add ing** and **ed** to each root word. **Write** the new words.

	ing	ed
1. skip	_____	_____
2. grin	_____	_____
3. drip	_____	_____
4. tug	_____	_____
5. ship	_____	_____
6. clap	_____	_____
7. knot	_____	_____

Read one inventor's log. **Circle** each word ending in **ing** or **ed**. **Write** the root word.

Monday: went jogging with Joe   _____

Tuesday: tapped maple trees for syrup   _____

Wednesday: canned string beans   _____

Thursday: went shopping with Elana   _____

Friday: went swimming and came up with an idea for a machine   _____

Write on Track   Work with a small group to invent a swimming machine. Jot down your ideas. Share your plans with classmates.

Here's a Hint!

Every **syllable** has a vowel sound. Sometimes an ending has a vowel sound and forms a syllable. Sometimes it does not.

us**es**—**2** vowel sounds—**2** syllables

us**ed**—**1** vowel sound—**1** syllable

Read each phrase. **Circle** the word ending in **s, es, ing,** or **ed. Write** the word under the correct heading.

	One Syllable	Two Syllables
1. often uses scrap material	_____	_____
2. builds a model	_____	_____
3. might have caused a problem	_____	_____
4. start making a plan	_____	_____
5. usually works on a team	_____	_____
6. carefully studies the problem	_____	_____
7. stopped to think	_____	_____
8. wanted to help	_____	_____
9. used a new method	_____	_____
10. makes a discovery	_____	_____
11. sketches an idea	_____	_____
12. got wrapped up in her work	_____	_____
13. will be changing the world	_____	_____

Work Together

Write a sentence using a two-syllable word with an ending. **Share** your sentence with a partner.

_____

_____

PHONICS ALIVE AT HOME Ask your child to read all the two-syllable words on the page to you.

Name _____

Add the ending to each root word and **write** the new word. Remember to make spelling changes. **Read** down to find the answer to the question.

1. chat + s   __ __ __ __ __

2. hatch + es   __ __ __ __ __ __ __

3. dry + ed   __ __ __ __ __

4. stay + s   __ __ __ __ __

5. try + s   __ __ __ __ __

6. play + ed   __ __ __ __ __ __

7. hum + ed   __ __ __ __ __ __

8. drip + ing   __ __ __ __ __ __ __

9. hope + ed   __ __ __ __ __

10. smile + ing __ __ __ __ __ __ __

11. cry + ing   __ __ __ __ __ __

12. plan + ed   __ __ __ __ __ __ __

13. name + ed   __ __ __ __ __

It's fun jumping and bouncing on this invention.
What is it?

_____

Write on Track

Learn more about this invention. Find out when it was invented and by whom. Write about it.

 Read the stories of two important inventions. **Add s, es, ing,** or **ed** to each root word and **write** a word to complete each sentence. Remember to make spelling changes.

The Light Bulb

Was it American Thomas Edison or Englishman

Joseph Swan who _____ the light bulb?
(invent)

The answer to the question _____ on
(depend)

whether you live in the United States or England.

Each inventor on his own _____ and found
(try)

a way to keep an electric light _____. So
(burn)

credit _____ to both inventors.
(belong)

The Traffic Light

Believe it or not, the first traffic light was

_____ for horses, not cars! One was
(invent)

installed in England in 1868 to keep horse carriages

from _____ people. The idea seemed good,
(hit)

but the light soon _____. Fifty years
(explode)

_____ before American Garret Morgan
(pass)

_____ a traffic light that worked.
(patent)

PHONICS Ask your child to read the stories to you and to point out the ending in **ALIVE AT HOME** each word he or she wrote.

Read and Write

Read the how-to article. **Think** about the steps for becoming an inventor. **Answer** the questions.

HOW TO BE AN Inventor

Use your brain and your imagination, and you can be an inventor. Here's how.

First, look for problems that need to be solved. For example, your CDs always fall on the floor, or your socks get mixed up in the wash. Brainstorm a list of possibilities.

Once you have a list, pick a problem to solve. Carefully think it over. Write down all possible solutions that pop into your head.

Now look at each solution. Cross out the ones that are silly or won't work. Circle the one that you'd like to try.

Make a drawing of your invention. List materials that you will need to make it. Then build a model with an adult's help.

When your model is done, try it out. If it works, you're an inventor!

1. What is the first step in becoming an inventor?

_____

_____

2. What should you do after you decide how to solve your problem?

_____

_____

Follow the steps to become an inventor. Decide on and plan an invention. Complete the application for a patent. Use one or more words from the box.

Writer's Tips

- Follow the directions for completing the application.
- Be precise. Make sure your reader understands what your invention does and how it works.
- Write neatly.

APPLICATION FOR A PATENT

To Whom It May Concern:

I, _____ , a resident of _____ , _____ ,
　　　　[name]　　　　　　　　　　　　　[city]　　　　　[state]

have invented _____ .
　　　　　　　　　　　　　　　[name of invention]

Purpose of Invention

Explain what your invention does and who would use it.

_____

_____

_____

_____

Description of Invention

Draw a picture of your invention in the space at the left.

Tell how it works.

_____

_____

_____

_____

I hereby apply for a patent.

Respectfully submitted,

_____　　_____
　　　　　　[signature]　　　　　　　　　　　　　[date]

added

adult's

attached

families

fixes

I'd

improves

inventing

kids'

lunches

solves

toys

158

Lesson 88 • Writing Contractions, Plurals, and Word Endings in Context
Comprehension: Identifying Steps in a Process

PHONICS ALIVE AT HOME

Ask your child to read his or her completed application to you, and to explain how to become an inventor.

Let's **read** and **talk** about a camp for inventors of the future.

Learn About Camp Invention

Are you interested in the world of inventors? If your answer is "yes," you may want to go to Camp Invention. This camp is a summer day camp for people who like to solve problems.

Camp Invention has different activity programs. In one, you'll get a chance to look at a few artists' work. For example, you can study Alexander Calder's mobiles to find out about metal objects moving in space. Then you'll have time to make a mobile of your own.

"What's Bugging You?" is another fun-filled program. While you're making a giant bug, you'll learn about insects' habits. What you discover may be useful to humans in the future.

Camp Invention is held in dozens of science centers and schools every summer.

Would you like to attend a program like Camp Invention? Explain why or why not.

 Check-Up Add **s** or **es, ing,** and **ed** to each root word. **Write** the new words.

	s or es	ing	ed
1. splash			
2. learn			
3. wave			
4. study			
5. scrub			
6. obey			

Check-Up Write the root word.

7. reaches _____	8. copies _____
9. baking _____	10. slipped _____
11. hurried _____	12. traces _____

Check-Up Add **ing** or **ed** to the root word to complete each sentence.

live 13. Mary Anderson _____ in Birmingham, Alabama.

visit 14. Some say that in 1902 she _____ New York City.

enjoy 15. For the most part, she _____ her visit.

ride 16. But she didn't like _____ in trolleys on rainy days.

stop 17. The driver could not wipe the windshields without _____.

solve 18. Ms. Anderson was good at _____ problems.

invent 19. She _____ a windshield wiper.

PHONICS ALIVE AT HOME Review this Check-Up with your child.

Space Campers' Song

3—2—I—and liftoff,
Campers, off we go!
Departing from the planet Earth,
We're fearless, don't you know?

Weightless as we rocket
Soaring in the sky,
Where nothing is impossible
And anyone can fly,

Adventurers in outer space
Where galaxies do churn—
*But don't forget about me, Mom,
In two weeks, I return.*

Anastasia Suen

Critical Thinking
What do you think is possible in outer space?
How do you think it feels to fly among the galaxies?

Name _____

Dear Family,

In this unit about outer space, your child will learn about suffixes, prefixes, and multisyllabic words. Share these definitions:

> **suffix:** a word part added to the end of a root word to change its meaning or make a new word (hope<u>ful</u>)
>
> **prefix:** a word part added to the beginning of a root word to change its meaning or make a new word (<u>re</u>tell)

- Read the poem on the reverse side. Talk about adventures a space camper has.

- Ask your child to find rhyming words such as **go** and **know** at the end of each pair of lines.

- Also search through the poem for words with suffixes, words with prefixes, and words with more than one syllable.

Apreciada Familia,

En esta unidad sobre el espacio los niños aprenderán sufijos, prefijos y palabras polisílabas. Compartan las siguientes definiciones:

> **sufijo:** letras que se añaden al final de una palabra base para cambiar su significado o hacer una nueva (hope<u>ful</u>)
>
> **prefijo:** letras que se añaden al principio de una palabra base para cambiar su significado o construir una nueva (<u>re</u>tell)

- Lean el poema en la página 161. Hablen de las aventuras en el campamento espacial.

- Pida al niño encontrar al final de cada verso palabras que riman tales como **go** y **know**.

- Busquen también palabras con sufijos y prefijos y palabras con más de una sílaba.

PROJECT

With your child, use tissue boxes to design two space stations. Mark one box "Space Station Suffix" and the other "Prefix Planet Port." When your child learns a new word with a suffix or a prefix, have him or her write the word on a slip of paper, underline the suffix or prefix, and then place the paper in the appropriate space station.

PROYECTO

Usen cajas de pañuelos desechables para diseñar dos estaciones espaciales. Marquen una "Estación Espacial Sufijo" y la otra "Puerto Planeta Prefijo". Cuando el niño aprenda una palabra con sufijo o prefijo pídale escribirla en un papel, subrayar el sufijo o prefijo y luego colocarla en la estación espacial adecuada.

Name _____

Here's a Hint! A **suffix** is a word part added to the end of a root word to change its meaning or make a new word.

hope + **ful** = hope**ful**   bright + **ly** = bright**ly**   near + **er** = near**er**

The suffix **ful** means "full of," as in **hopeful**. The suffix **less** means "without," as in **hopeless**. The suffix **ness** means "a state of being," as in **darkness**. Add **ful, less,** or **ness** to the root word and **write** the word that goes with each definition.

1. full of **hope** _____	2. without **hope** _____	3. being **dark** _____
4. without **sun** _____	5. full of **cheer** _____	6. being **light** _____
7. being **good** _____	8. without **weight** _____	9. full of **color** _____

Add **ful, less,** or **ness** to each word in **bold** print so that the sentence makes sense. **Write** the new word.

10. The spacecraft took off on a **cloud** morning.   _____

11. The **bright** of the sun lit up the sky.   _____

12. The astronauts were **hope** that they would reach the moon.   _____

13. Several days later, they made a **grace** landing.   _____

14. The brave astronauts were **fear** in the face of danger.   _____

15. It's no wonder everyone praised their **great**.   _____

The suffix **ly** means "in a certain way." **Brightly** means "in a bright way." The suffix **y** means "full of" or "having." **Rainy** means "having rain." **Write** the meaning of each word with **ly** or **y**.

1. brightly _____

2. rainy _____

3. safely _____

4. thirsty _____

5. speedy _____

6. clearly _____

7. snowy _____

8. completely _____

9. softly _____

Work Together Work with a partner. **Add ly** or **y** to the root word to answer each question.

bright 10. How does the sun shine? _____

rock 11. What is the moon like? _____

quick 12. How do shooting stars move? _____

loud 13. How do crowds cheer? _____

salt 14. What is the ocean like? _____

dust 15. What is the planet Mars like? _____

brave 16. How does a space explorer act? _____

wind 17. What is a hurricane like? _____

slow 18. How does the moon travel around Earth? _____

Write on Track Write two or three questions that can be answered with words that end in **ly** or **y**.

PHONICS ALIVE AT HOME With your child, take turns making up your own questions that can be answered with words that end in **y** or **ly**.

Name _____

Here's a Hint! The suffix **er** is added to a root word to compare two things. The suffix **est** is added to compare more than two things. Sometimes you need to make spelling changes before adding **er** or **est**.

big + **er** = big**ger**   big + **est** = big**gest**
easy + **er** = eas**ier**   easy + **est** = eas**iest**

Compare the sizes of the planets. **Add er** or **est** to the root word **big** and **write** the new word. Remember to make spelling changes.

Planet	Size Across in Miles
Uranus	31,800
Saturn	74,900
Jupiter	88,800

Uranus is a **big** planet.

1. Saturn is a ___bigger___ planet.

2. Jupiter is the ___biggest___ planet.

Add er and **est** to each root word. **Write** the new words. Remember to make spelling changes.

	er	**est**
3. easy	easier	easiest
4. near	nearer	nearest
5. hot	hotter	hottest
6. high	higher	highest
7. sad	sadder	saddest
8. happy	happier	happiest
9. early	earlier	earliest

Write on Track Find out about the sizes of the planets Venus, Mars, and Mercury. Write three sentences comparing them. Use the words **small, smaller,** and **smallest.**

Suffixes

The suffix **en** means "make." **Darken** means "make dark." The suffixes **able** and **ible** mean "can be." **Washable** means "can be washed." **Collectible** means "can be collected." **Write** the meaning of each word.

1. darken   _make dark_

2. washable   _can be washed_

3. collectible   _can be collected_

4. soften   _make soft_

5. readable   _able to read_

6. sharpen   _make sharp_

7. resistible   _can be resisted_

8. enjoyable   _can be enjoyable_

9. straighten   _make straight_

Write a word from above to complete each sentence.

Things to Do at Space Camp

✔ Don't forget to _straighten_ your cabin.

✔ Wash your clothes every week. They're all _washable_.

✔ _Sharpen_ your pencils and write home often.

✔ Write neatly. Make sure your postcards are _readable_.

✔ Bring back moon rocks. They're _enjoyable_.

✔ Have an _resistible_ time.

Write on Track

With a classmate, make a list of collectibles, or things that can be collected. You might start with "moon rocks."

PHONICS
ALIVE AT HOME

Together, look in a newspaper or book for words that end with the suffixes **en, able,** or **ible.**

The suffix **ment** means "a state of being" or "the act or result of." **Movement** is the act or result of moving. The suffix **ion** means "the result of." An **Invention** is the result of inventing. **Fill in** the circle next to the suffix that can be added to each root word. **Write** the new word.

1. move   ○ ment   ○ ion   _____

2. invent   ○ ment   ○ ion   _____

3. amaze   ○ ment   ○ ion   _____

4. correct   ○ ment   ○ ion   _____

5. measure   ○ ment   ○ ion   _____

6. govern   ○ ment   ○ ion   _____

7. direct   ○ ment   ○ ion   _____

8. elect   ○ ment   ○ ion   _____

9. pave   ○ ment   ○ ion   _____

Work Together

Add ment or **ion** to the root word to complete each sentence. Take turns **reading** the sentences with a partner.

settle   10. Welcome to the first _____ on the moon.

excite   11. Your visit has created a lot of _____.

move   12. You'll notice that _____ is easy.

entertain   13. Free floating is a favorite form of _____.

construct   14. Permanent housing is still under _____.

invent   15. The dome you'll stay in is a new _____.

protect   16. It provides _____ against heat and cold.

improve   17. It's an _____ over a space station.

collect   18. This museum houses our _____ of metals.

attract   19. It's an _____ most visitors enjoy seeing.

Suffixes

The suffixes **er, or,** and **ist** mean "someone who." A **farmer** is someone who farms. An **actor** is someone who acts. A **violinist** is someone who plays a violin. **Write** each word in the box under the correct heading.

actor	boxer	builder	cartoonist	conductor	farmer
inventor	journalist	sailor	teacher	tourist	violinist

1. Words with **er**	2. Words with **or**	3. Words with **ist**
_____	_____	_____
_____	_____	_____
_____	_____	_____
_____	_____	_____

Write the word from above that fits each clue.

4. He had the idea of the first telescope. _____

5. She would like to tour Mars. _____

6. You'll see this person in the movies. _____

7. This person grows vegetables. _____

8. She draws a comic strip. _____

9. He writes for the newspaper. _____

10. You'll see this person in the classroom. _____

11. This person leads an orchestra. _____

12. You'll see this person in a boxing ring. _____

13. This person plays the violin. _____

14. This person sails the seas. _____

Write on Track

Write a word with **er, or,** or **ist** that can be used to describe you.

PHONICS ALIVE AT HOME Ask your child to write clues for the words **artist, director,** and **photographer.**

Word Strategy You can use a suffix you know to help you read an unknown word. **ful**   hope**ful**   thought**ful**

Say the suffix at the beginning of each row. **Circle** the words that end with the same suffix.

1.	**ful**	hopeful	hoping	thoughtful	thoughtless
2.	**less**	dampness	weightless	cheerful	shapeless
3.	**ness**	pointless	closeness	sickness	tightest
4.	**ly**	safely	safer	thirsty	sweetly
5.	**y**	squeaky	kindly	rocky	rocket
6.	**er**	lighter	louder	little	lightest
7.	**est**	warmest	wanted	greatest	slower

Interview an astronaut. **Write** a circled word from above to complete each question. Use the suffix clues to help you. **Write** two interview questions of your own.

less   **8.** How does it feel to be _____ in space?

ness   **9.** Did you ever experience motion _____?

est   **10.** What was your spacecraft's _____ speed?

er   **11.** Was the noise _____ during blastoff or touchdown?

y   **12.** Is the moon's surface really _____?

ly   **13.** How did you feel after landing _____?

ful   **14.** Are you _____ that someday we'll live in space?

15. _____

_____

16. _____

_____

Syllables

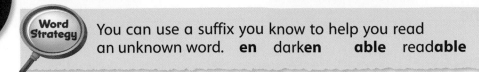

Word Strategy You can use a suffix you know to help you read an unknown word. **en** dark**en** **able** read**able**

Say each root word and suffix. **Add** the suffix to the root word to **write** a new word.

1.
light + en _____

bright + en _____

2.
bend + able _____

wear + able _____

3.
collect + ible _____

resist + ible _____

4.
place + ment _____

agree + ment _____

5.
subtract + ion _____

suggest + ion _____

6.
lead + er _____

sing + er _____

7.
conduct + or _____

visit + or _____

8.
guitar + ist _____

novel + ist _____

Write a word from above to answer each question.

9. What two-syllable word is a kind of entertainer? _____

10. What three-syllable word is another word for **guest?** _____

11. What two-syllable word is the act of placing? _____

12. What three-syllable word is the opposite of **addition?** _____

13. What two-syllable word means "make light"? _____

14. What three-syllable word is an author? _____

15. What four-syllable word means "can be resisted"? _____

16. What three-syllable word means "can be bent"? _____

PHONICS ALIVE AT HOME Ask your child to point out the words he or she wrote in items 1–8 that have more than two syllables.

Name _____

⭐ **Read** about some visitors from space. **Answer** the questions.

Visitors from Space

It's a dark night. The stars are shining brightly. You hear a knock and open your door. To your amazement, in float several tourists from space. What might they be like? Before you guess, it would be helpful to know something about their home planet.

Let's say your visitors come from a snowy planet—the planet farthest from the sun. They might have hairy bodies for protection against the cold.

Let's say the travelers come from a large planet—one that has stronger gravity than Earth. Then they might feel almost weightless. They'd be light on their feet and able to jump higher than you.

Will they definitely have feet? It's questionable. What do you think?

1. Why might space visitors have hairy bodies?

_____

_____

2. How might coming from a large planet affect the visitors' movement on Earth?

_____

_____

3. Do you think it's possible for space visitors to be exactly like humans?

Why or why not?

_____

_____

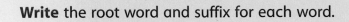 **Write** the root word and suffix for each word.

	Root Word	Suffix
1. measurement	_____	_____
2. weightless	_____	_____
3. breakable	_____	_____
4. inventor	_____	_____
5. collectible	_____	_____
6. tourist	_____	_____
7. darkness	_____	_____
8. teacher	_____	_____

 Fill in the circle next to the word that makes sense in each sentence.

9. The planet Venus _____ the night sky.
   ○ brightness　　　○ brightly　　　○ brightens

10. Of all the planets, it is _____ to Earth.
    ○ nearly　　　○ nearer　　　○ nearest

11. It spins in the opposite _____.
    ○ direction　　　○ directed　　　○ directly

12. It is _____ covered by a thick layer of clouds.
    ○ completely　　　○ completed　　　○ completeness

13. The ground below the clouds is _____.
    ○ rocked　　　○ rocker　　　○ rocky

14. It's much _____ on Venus than it is on Earth.
    ○ hot　　　○ hotter　　　○ hottest

PHONICS ALIVE AT HOME Review this Check-Up with your child.

Here's a Hint! A **prefix** is a word part added to the beginning of a root word to change its meaning or make a new word.

re + tell = **re**tell   **in** + correct = **in**correct   **pre** + pay = **pre**pay

The prefix **re** means "again" or "back," as in **retell** and **return**. The prefixes **un** and **dis** mean "not" or "do the opposite of," as in **unsafe** and **disagree**. Add **re, un,** or **dis** to the root word and **write** the word that goes with each definition.

1. **tell** again	2. not **honest**	3. **turn** back
_____	_____	_____
4. not **known**	5. **build** again	6. not **safe**
_____	_____	_____
7. the opposite of **obey**	8. the opposite of **load**	9. the opposite of **agree**
_____	_____	_____

Add **re, un,** or **dis** to each word in **bold** print so that the sentence makes sense. **Write** the new word.

10. I checked and then **checked** the facts.   _____

11. I worked hard to **cover** information.   _____

12. But my report on black holes **appeared!**   _____

13. I've looked, but I'm **able** to find it.   _____

14. My teacher **likes** excuses.   _____

15. I guess that I'll have to **write** it.   _____

The prefixes **in** and **im** mean "not." **Incorrect** means "not correct." **Impossible** means "not possible." **Add in** or **im** to each root word. **Write** the new word.

1. Add **in**

correct _____

visible _____

complete _____

formal _____

expensive _____

active _____

2. Add **im**

possible _____

polite _____

pure _____

patient _____

perfect _____

mature _____

Work Together **Write** a word from above to complete each sentence. **Compare** answers with a partner.

3. A person who is not patient is _____.

4. A toy that is not expensive is _____.

5. Something that is not perfect is _____.

6. Someone who is not polite is _____.

7. A job that has not been completed is _____.

8. Something that cannot be seen is _____.

9. A volcano that is not active is _____.

10. Water that is not pure is _____.

11. An answer that is not correct is _____.

12. A person who is not mature is _____.

13. Something that is not possible is _____.

14. A party that is not formal is _____.

Write on Track Write a sentence to describe something that is impossible on Earth, but possible in space.

The prefix **pre** means "before." **Prepay** means "pay before." The prefix **de** means "remove." **Defrost** means "remove frost from." The prefix **mis** means "in a wrong or bad way." **Misspell** means "spell wrong." **Write** each word under the correct heading.

decode	defrost	mislabel	prepay	misspell	preview
defang	pretest	dethrone	mistreat	misuse	prewash

I. Words with **pre**	**2.** Words with **de**	**3.** Words with **mis**
_____	_____	_____
_____	_____	_____
_____	_____	_____
_____	_____	_____

 Write a word from above to complete each sentence.

4. When you test something in advance, you _____ it.

5. When you remove frost from a windshield, you _____ it.

6. When you treat a pet badly, you _____ it.

7. When you use a knife as a fork, you _____ it.

8. When you pay for something in advance, you _____.

9. When you remove or break a secret code, you _____.

10. When you wash something beforehand, you _____ it.

11. When you spell a word incorrectly, you _____ it.

12. When you remove the queen from her throne, you _____ her.

13. When you skim a book before reading it, you _____ it.

 **Write on Track**

Write a sentence to explain why the word **prefix** begins with **pre**.

Word Strategy You can use a prefix you know to help you read an unknown word. **re** **re**check **re**read

Say the prefix at the beginning of each row. **Circle** the words that begin with the same prefix.

1.	**re**	(redo)	(reread)	preheat	defrost
2.	**un**	ugly	(unhappy)	onion	(unwrap)
3.	**dis**	describe	listen	(dislike)	(displease)
4.	**in**	(inactive)	impolite	(indirect)	imperfect
5.	**im**	(impossible)	inexpensive	(improper)	unknown
6.	**pre**	(preschool)	retake	repay	(prehistoric)
7.	**de**	(debug)	preview	(declaw)	distrust
8.	**mis**	middle	disobey	(mislead)	(mistook)

Write a circled word from above to answer each question.

9. What two-syllable word means "read again"? _reread_

10. What three-syllable word is the opposite of **direct?** _indirect_

11. What four-syllable word describes early times in history? _prehistoric_

12. What two-syllable word means "remove the claws of"? _declaw_

13. What three-syllable word is another word for **sad?** _unhappy_

14. What four-syllable word is the opposite of **possible?** _impossible_

15. What two-syllable word is a form of the word **mistake?** _mistook_

16. What two-syllable word is the opposite of **please?** _displease_

Write on Track Sort the words with prefixes into three lists: Words with Two Syllables, Words with Three Syllables, Words with Four Syllables.

PHONICS ALIVE AT HOME Ask your child to write questions about the words with prefixes that are not circled in items 1–8.

Name _Wesley Lim_

Write a word with a prefix for each clue. Use a prefix from the box. Then **read** down to find the answer to the question.

| re | un | dis | in | im | pre | de | mis |

1. cook before   _p r e c o o k_

2. not correct   _i n c o r r e c t_

3. the opposite of **cover**   _u n c o v e r_

4. spell in a wrong way   _m i s s p e l l_

5. tell again   _r e t e l l_

6. heat before   _p r e h e a t_

7. the opposite of **like**   _d i s l i k e_

8. remove the claws of   _d e c l a w_

9. not patient   _i n p a t i e n t_

10. treat badly   _m i s t r e a t_

11. not pure   _i m p u r e_

12. remove the code   _d e c o d e_

13. the opposite of **wrap**   _u n w r a p_

14. the opposite of **obey**   _d i s o b e y_

What are groups of bright stars that form shapes in the sky?

constellations

Check-Up **Write** the prefix and root word for each word.

	Prefix	Root Word
1. decode	_____	_____
2. misuse	_____	_____
3. disobey	_____	_____
4. prewash	_____	_____
5. impolite	_____	_____
6. unknown	_____	_____
7. invisible	_____	_____
8. rebuild	_____	_____

Check-Up **Fill in** the circle next to the word that makes sense in each sentence.

9. The sun was formed in _____ times.
   ○ prehistoric   ○ inexpensive   ○ pretest

10. It's _____ to look directly at it.
    ○ unable   ○ unsafe   ○ impatient

11. It's _____ to live without it.
    ○ inactive   ○ unhappy   ○ impossible

12. During an eclipse, the sun seems to _____.
    ○ disagree   ○ declaw   ○ disappear

13. It _____ a few minutes later.
    ○ rechecks   ○ returns   ○ prepays

14. Long ago people _____ an eclipse for a dragon eating the sun!
    ○ mistook   ○ mistreat   ○ mislead

PHONICS ALIVE AT HOME Review this Check-Up with your child.

Name _____

Here's a Hint! If a word has two or more consonants between two vowels, usually divide the word between the first two consonants.

ex-pect   h**un-dre**d
VC CV   VC CCV

⭐ **Write** each word, dividing it into syllables with a hyphen.

1. expect _____	**2.** hundred _____
3. surface _____	**4.** person _____
5. mission _____	**6.** shelter _____
7. success _____	**8.** surround _____
9. orbit _____	**10.** correct _____
11. common _____	**12.** surprise _____

⭐ **Write** a word from above to complete each sentence.

13. Cosmonaut Yuri Gagarin was the first _____ to circle Earth in 1961.

14. A year later, astronaut John Glenn went into _____ .

15. Seven years later, Neil Armstrong went on a _____ to the moon.

16. Scientists _____ that in the future astronauts will visit other planets.

17. Someday space travel may become as _____ as airplane travel.

Here's a Hint!

If a word has one consonant between two vowels, first divide the word before the consonant. The first vowel sound will usually be long. If you still don't recognize the word, divide after the consonant. The vowel sound will usually be short.

fu-ture   plan-ets
V CV   VC V

Write each word, dividing it into syllables with a hyphen.

1. future _____	2. planets _____
3. nature _____	4. solar _____
5. cabin _____	6. metal _____
7. climate _____	8. silence _____
9. moment _____	10. frozen _____
11. panel _____	12. travel _____
13. shiver _____	14. models _____

Work Together

Write a word from above to complete each sentence.
Take turns **reading** the sentences with a partner.

15. The museum has exhibits on both past and _____ space flights.

16. One room is set up like the _____ of a spacecraft.

17. Visitors can sit behind the control _____.

18. Another room displays all the planets in the _____ system.

19. The scale _____ are built to show the planets' sizes.

20. Jupiter is bigger than all the other _____ put together!

PHONICS ALIVE AT HOME For items 1–14, ask your child to read each word and say if the first vowel sound is long or short.

Name _____

Here's a Hint! Divide a compound word between its word parts.

moon-walk **ice-berg**

⭐ **Write** each compound word, dividing it into syllables with a hyphen.

1. moonwalk _____	**2.** iceberg _____
3. blastoff _____	**4.** sunspot _____
5. spacesuit _____	**6.** daytime _____
7. postcard _____	**8.** footprints _____
9. daydream _____	**10.** touchdown _____
11. snowball _____	**12.** starlight _____
13. spacecraft _____	**14.** outside _____

⭐ **Write** the compound word from above that fits each clue.

15. This is a dark spot on the sun. _____

16. This is another word for **spaceship.** _____

17. This is a walk on the moon. _____

18. This is what Neil Armstrong left on the moon. _____

19. This is the launching of a spacecraft. _____

20. This is the landing of a spacecraft. _____

Here's a Hint! If a word ends in a consonant followed by **le**, the word is usually divided before the consonant.

mid-**dle**   twin-**kle**

Read about a late night event. **Underline** the words in the selection that end in a consonant followed by **le**. Then **write** each underlined word below, dividing it into syllables with a hyphen.

A Star in the Night

It was the middle of the night. I looked up at the sky and saw a star twinkle. Suddenly a small object no bigger than a pebble fell to Earth. It landed with a splash in a puddle of rainwater. Something began to wriggle out.

It was quite a struggle! Finally, a tiny, fuzzy snake with two heads and a single body appeared. Each head looked like a round, blue marble. I tried not to startle the creature. I heard it gurgle softly.

Just then I felt Mom's gentle hand touch my cheek. I turned to point to the star snake with the double head.

_____   _____   _____

_____   _____   _____

_____   _____   _____

_____   _____   _____

What happens next? **Write** an ending to the story.

_____

_____

_____

_____

_____

PHONICS ALIVE AT HOME Together, read the story. Ask your child to read his or her ending to you.

Name _____

Here's a Hint! If a word has an ending with a vowel sound, the word is usually divided between the root word and the ending.

splash-**es**   thrill-**ing**   blast-**ed**

 Write each word, dividing it into syllables with a hyphen.

1. splashes _____		**2.** thrilling _____
3. blasted _____		**4.** reaches _____
5. landed _____		**6.** touring _____
7. passes _____		**8.** wanted _____
9. flying _____		**10.** mixes _____
11. waited _____		**12.** missing _____

 Write a word from above to complete each sentence. **Read** Davey's note.

Dear Mom and Dad,

I love _____ the solar system. We're

_____ at incredible speeds. By the time

this note _____ you, we'll have

_____ on Mars. You know I've always

_____ to leave my footprints there!

I'm having a blast!

Davey

Here's a Hint! If a word has a suffix, the word is usually divided between the root word and the suffix.
hope-**ful**   weight-**less**

Read each phrase and **circle** the word with a suffix.
Write the word, dividing it into syllables with a hyphen.

1. hopeful about the future   _____

2. feel weightless in space   _____

3. freeze in the darkness   _____

4. bravely face the unknown   _____

5. a rocky surface   _____

6. smaller in size   _____

7. the brightness of the stars   _____

8. darken the skies   _____

9. the movement of the planets   _____

10. the best teacher   _____

11. a sailor among the stars   _____

12. a tourist on Earth   _____

13. a rainless planet   _____

14. the greatest distance   _____

15. splash down safely   _____

16. a graceful landing   _____

17. a dirty snowball   _____

18. sharpen the focus   _____

Write on Track How do you divide a word that ends with the suffix **able** or **ible**?
Divide the word **readable.** Use what you know about suffixes and words that end in a consonant followed by **le.**

 PHONICS ALIVE AT HOME Together, scan a newspaper column for hyphenated words with suffixes. Notice how they are divided.

Name _____

Here's a Hint! Divide a word with a prefix between the prefix and the root word.
re-check   **un**-known

Read each phrase and **circle** the word with a prefix.
Write the word, dividing it into syllables with a hyphen.

1. check and recheck the facts _____

2. learn about the unknown _____

3. dislike the darkness _____

4. avoid impure water _____

5. prepay for the flight _____

6. can't decode the message _____

7. misplace the tickets _____

8. an incorrect answer _____

Work Together **Choose** five words you wrote above and use each in a sentence.
Share your sentences with a partner.

9. _____
_____

10. _____
_____

11. _____
_____

12. _____
_____

13. _____
_____

Review

Write each word, dividing it into syllables with a hyphen.

VCCV Words

1. number _____
2. command _____
3. purpose _____
4. danger _____

VCV Words

5. travel _____
6. silence _____
7. nature _____
8. figure _____

Compound Words

9. spacecraft _____
10. fireworks _____
11. earthquake _____
12. daydream _____

Words Ending in **le**

13. pebble _____
14. giggle _____
15. people _____
16. single _____

Words Ending in **es, ing, ed**

17. matches _____
18. speeding _____
19. waited _____
20. headed _____

Words with Suffixes and Prefixes

21. artist _____
22. brighten _____
23. preview _____
24. rebuild _____

PHONICS ALIVE AT HOME

Ask your child to explain how he or she divided up each set of words.

Name _____

 Spell, Write, and Tell

Read the phrases in the box. **Say** and **spell** each word in **bold** print. **Repeat** the word. **Sort** the words.

a **better** view

departing from Earth

disappear into a black hole

an **impossible** plan

invisible to the naked eye

the biggest **planet**

in **prehistoric** times

beyond the **solar** system

launched a **spaceship**

streaking across the sky

a good **suggestion**

the moon's rocky **surface**

a **twinkle** in the darkness

explore the **unknown**

Two Syllables	Three Syllables
_____	_____
_____	_____
_____	_____
_____	**Four Syllables**
_____	_____
_____	_____
_____	_____

Spell, Write, and Tell

Imagine that you've discovered a new planet. **Write** a speech in which you greet visitors to your planet. In your speech, use one or more of the words in the box. **Deliver** your speech to the class.

better	departing	disappear	impossible	invisible
	planet	prehistoric	solar	spaceship
streaking	suggestion	surface	twinkle	unknown

_____

_____

_____

_____

_____

_____

_____

_____

_____

_____

_____

_____

_____

MEET THE STARS

PHONICS ALIVE AT HOME

Accept an invitation to tour the new planet. Ask your child to deliver his or her speech.

Read and Write **Read** the conversation between a passenger and a driver on a bus traveling in space. **Think** about what the passenger says. **Answer** the questions.

Aboard the Space Bus

Passenger: I can't believe I'm a space traveler! It's thrilling. Driver, what's the first stop?

Driver: Our spacecraft is scheduled to pass Mercury. Mercury is the hottest planet. Do you know why?

Passenger: Because it's nearest the sun. So I guess it's unsafe to land there.

Driver: Right. After Mercury, our spaceship will travel toward Venus. Venus is the planet closest to Earth.

Passenger: Then can we go to Mars? I've heard that people live there.

Driver: That's doubtful, but we'll have an enjoyable visit, anyhow.

Passenger: Then can we go to Jupiter? It's bigger than all the other planets. And after that, can we go to—

Driver: Calm down, ma'am! Don't be impatient! It's impossible to visit all the planets in one trip. We need to return to Earth for more fuel.

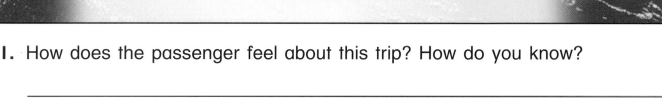

1. How does the passenger feel about this trip? How do you know?

_____

_____

2. How would you describe the driver on this space bus?

_____

_____

Imagine that it's the year 3000. You and a friend are on a Space Bus, heading for vacation on a faraway planet. **Write** a conversation that you have. Use one or more words from the box.

Writer's Tips

• Talk about what you see or hear.
• Tell where you are headed.
• Use the kind of language that you use when you talk with friends.

amazement	brightness	cloudless	colorful	easier	happiest
impossible	invisible	loudly	preview	tourist	windy

PHONICS ALIVE AT HOME

Together, read the conversation that your child wrote. Each of you can take a part.

Let's **read** and **talk** about space shuttles.

Learn About Space Shuttles

You hear a noise louder than thunder. The rocket carrying the space shuttle rises. Quickly the rocket disappears into a cloudless sky.

A space shuttle is a spacecraft that can be used over and over. Since the *Columbia* blasted off in 1981, there have been many space-shuttle flights. In 1983, Sally Ride was a crew member on the shuttle *Challenger.* She became the first American woman in space.

A shuttle can hold up to seven people. It can carry about 65,000 pounds of equipment. Shuttle crew members use this equipment to perform experiments in space. They check and recheck test results. They launch satellites that gather and send information to scientists on Earth. Shuttle crews also capture and fix broken satellites.

What would you like most about being a crew member on a space shuttle?

Lesson 113 • Suffixes, Prefixes, and Multisyllabic Words in Context
Comprehension: Relating to Personal Experiences
Developing Fluency

Check-Up **Write** each word, dividing it into syllables with a hyphen.

1. swiftly _____	2. object _____
3. frozen _____	4. thrilling _____
5. wriggle _____	6. sunshine _____
7. collect _____	8. crater _____
9. shorten _____	10. decode _____
11. moonlight _____	12. reaches _____
13. review _____	14. gentle _____

Check-Up **Circle** and **write** the two-syllable word that completes each sentence.

15. A planetarium is _____ any theater you've ever seen.
    dislike   unlike   different

16. The ceiling curves over you like a(n) _____ sky.
    endless   ending   dark

17. Stars _____ as though you are really outside.
    shine   wiggle   twinkle

18. The moon and the _____ surround you.
    planets   stars   planes

19. You can watch the _____ of a comet.
    silence   light   movement

20. Meteors go _____ across the sky.
    streak   streaking   streaky

PHONICS *ALIVE AT HOME* Review this Check-Up with your child.

Have You Ever Seen?

Have you ever seen a sheet on a river bed?
Or a single hair from a hammer's head?
Has the foot of a mountain any toes?
And is there a pair of garden hose?

Does the needle ever wink its eye?
Why doesn't the wing of a building fly?
Can you tickle the ribs of a parasol?
Or open the trunk of a tree at all?

Are the teeth of a rake ever going to bite?
Have the hands of a clock any left or right?
Can the garden plot be deep and dark?
And what is the sound of the birch's bark?

Anonymous

Critical Thinking How would you answer each question in the poem?
What do you think makes the poem fun to read?

Lesson 114 • Synonyms, Antonyms, Homonyms, and Dictionary Skills
Poetry: Word Play and Rhyme
Developing Fluency

Name _____

Dear Family,

In this unit that's just for fun, your child will study words and their meanings. Share these definitions:

> **synonyms:** words that have the same or nearly the same meaning **(sound/noise)**
>
> **antonyms:** words that have the opposite meaning **(dark/light)**
>
> **homonyms:** words that sound the same, but have different spellings and meanings **(eye/I)**

- Read the poem on the reverse side. Talk about words with more than one meaning, for example, **bed,** and how they make the poem funny.

- Call attention to the rhyming words, such as **bed** and **head.**

- Have fun with words in the poem. Think of a synonym for **seen. (noticed)** Find a pair of antonyms in the last stanza. **(left** and **right)** Think of a homonym for **pair. (pear)**

Apreciada Familia,

En esta unidad que es sólo para divertirse, los niños estudiarán palabras y su significado. Compartan estas definiciones:

> **sinónimos:** palabras que tienen el mismo significado **(sound/noise)**
>
> **antónimos:** palabras que significan lo opuesto **(dark/light)**
>
> **homónimos:** palabras que tienen el mismo sonido pero diferente significado y se escriben diferente **(eye/I)**

- Lean el poema en la página 193. Hablen sobre palabras con más de un significado cómo por ejemplo: **bed,** y como hacen que el poema sea divertido.

- Señale a las palabras que riman tales como: **bed** y **head.**

- Diviértanse con las palabras en el poema. Piensen en un sinónimo para **seen. (noticed)** Busque un par de antónimos en la última estrofa. **(left** y **right)** Piensen un homónimo para **pair. (pear)**

PROJECT

With your child, begin a "Word of the Day" campaign. Each day help your child find an unusual word in the dictionary. Write the word on an index card and display it for the day. Encourage your child to use the word in conversation.

Word of the Day: defrost

PROYECTO

Inicie una campaña "Palabra del día". Todos los días ayude al niño a encontrar una palabra poco común en el diccionario. Escriba la palabra en una tarjeta 3 X 5 y exhíbala durante un día. Anime al niño a usar la palabra en una conversación.

Name _____

Here's a Hint! **Antonyms** are words that have opposite or nearly opposite meanings.
yesterday—tomorrow

Draw a line from a word in the first column to its antonym in the second column.

1.			2.		
yesterday	beginning		clean	first	
winter	tomorrow		slowly	early	
end	summer		late	quickly	
empty	full		last	dirty	
3.			4.		
hello	thin		sharp	none	
come	go		above	dull	
thick	good-bye		all	west	
remember	forget		east	below	

Edit each sentence. **Replace** the word in **bold** print with its antonym from above.

yesterday
5. My alarm didn't ring ~~tomorrow.~~
   ^

6. I was afraid I'd be **early** for school.

7. I got dressed **slowly.**

8. I yelled **hello** as I ran out the door.

9. Whew! I was the **last** one at the bus stop.

10. "Don't you **forget?**" Dad called out to me.

11. "Today is the **end** of summer vacation."

12. "**Go** back home!"

Write on Track Write a message in which you say the opposite of what you mean. Challenge a classmate to use antonyms to decode it.

Write an antonym from the box for each clue word.
Read down to find a tongue twister that answers the question.

after	asleep	cool	daughter	difficult	east	few	healthy
inside	large	neat	old	safe	slow	strong	subtract	tight

1. west   — __ __ __ __

2. awake   — __ __ __ __ __

3. messy   — __ __ __ __

4. small   — __ __ __ __

5. before   — __ __ __ __

6. easy   — __ __ __ __ __ __ __ __

7. add   — __ __ __ __ __ __ __ __

8. son   — __ __ __ __ __ __ __

9. fast   — __ __ __ __

10. loose   — __ __ __ __ __

11. many   — __ __ __

12. new   — __ __ __

13. warm   — __ __ __

14. dangerous   — __ __ __

15. outside   — __ __ __ __ __

16. weak   — __ __ __ __ __

17. sick   — __ __ __ __ __ __

What do you call a lobster that won't share?

_____

At random, ask your child to name an antonym for each clue word in the box.

Here's a Hint! **Homonyms** are words that sound the same, but have different spellings and meanings.
some—sum

 Write a homonym from the box for each word.

| cents | eight | hole | know | not | sum | weight | where |

1. some _____

2. whole _____

3. ate _____

4. knot _____

5. wait _____

6. sense _____

7. wear _____

8. no _____

 Unscramble the letters to **write** the word that completes each sentence. The answer will be a homonym of the clue word.

lWodu 9. _____ you like to write a riddle?
(Wood)

hosoce 10. First _____ a word with a homonym to be the answer.
(chews)

owt 11. Think about the meanings of the _____ words.
(too)

oyur 12. Make sure _____ question uses both meanings.
(you're)

erHe 13. _____ is an example.
(Hear)

uns 14. What colors are the _____ and the wind?
(son)

ulbe 15. The sun rose and the wind _____.
(blew)

 **Write on Track** Follow the directions above to write your own riddle.

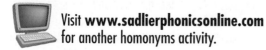 Visit www.sadlierphonicsonline.com for another homonyms activity.

Work Together Circle the pair of homonyms in each sentence. **Write** a definition for each circled word. Compare definitions with a partner.

1. The flu made me feel (weak) for about a (week.)
   <u>weak: not strong</u>
   <u>week: seven days</u>

2. Do you like the tale about a monkey without a tail?
   _____
   _____

3. Your nose always knows when it's time for dinner.
   _____
   _____

4. Did you write the right answers in the puzzle?
   _____
   _____

5. Julio threw the ball so hard it went through the window.
   _____
   _____

6. Each of the girls won one game of checkers.
   _____
   _____

7. Dad and Omar rode their bikes on the country road.
   _____
   _____

PHONICS ALIVE AT HOME Together, use each of these homonym pairs in a sentence: **ate, eight; hole, whole; cents, sense.**

Name _____

Spell, Write, and Tell

Read the phrases in the box. **Say** and **spell** each word in **bold** print. **Repeat** the word. **Sort** the words. **Write** two pairs of synonyms, two pairs of antonyms, and three pairs of homonyms.

in the **beginning**

dollars and **cents**

a **clever** trick

the **end** of the story

a **hole** in the bucket

inside the house

an **odd** feeling

play **outside**

makes no **sense**

a **smart** dog

a **strange** sound

wagged its **tail**

told a **tale**

ate the **whole** thing

Synonyms

_____ _____

_____ _____

Antonyms

_____ _____

_____ _____

Homonyms

_____ _____

_____ _____

_____ _____

Visit **www.sadlierphonicsonline.com** for more synonyms, antonyms, and homonyms.

Spelling and Writing

Have fun with words. **Write** a funny story, a silly song, or a rollicking rhyme. **Write** anything you'd like! Use one or more of the words in the box. **Share** your work with a friend.

beginning	cents	clever	end	hole	inside	odd
outside	sense	smart	strange	tail	tale	whole

PHONICS ALIVE AT HOME

Read your child's work. Then write something together. Use one or more spelling words.

Read the book review. Think about how the reader felt about the book. **Answer** the questions.

Read and Write

Guppies in Tuxedos
by Marvin Terban

Did you know that guppies are named for R. J. Lechmere Guppy? He discovered the fish on a South American island. And formal suits are called tuxedos for Tuxedo Park, New York. That's the place they were first worn.

You will find the story of the words "guppies" and "tuxedos" in *Guppies in Tuxedos* by Marvin Terban. It's a book of eponyms. An eponym is a person or place that becomes a word.

I was amazed to learn all the words that are eponyms. Leotards are named for a circus performer. Thursday gets its name from Thor, the Scandinavian god of thunder. Hamburgers come from the city of Hamburg in Germany.

My favorite eponym is "teddy" in teddy bear. Believe it or not, "teddy" is Theodore Roosevelt—the 26th president of the United States!

To find out about other eponyms, read *Guppies in Tuxedos*. You won't be disappointed.

I. What is an eponym?

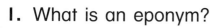

_____

2. Did the reader enjoy this book? Explain your answer.

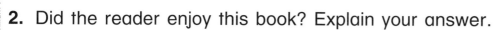

_____

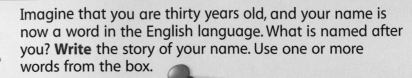

Imagine that you are thirty years old, and your name is now a word in the English language. What is named after you? **Write** the story of your name. Use one or more words from the box.

Writer's Tips

- Choose a category—food, clothing, places, or things—and decide what will be named after you.
- Start by telling what the new word based on your name means.
- Explain how the word came to be named after you.

difficult	forget	hear	know	quickly	slowly
easy	remember	here	no	hard	understand

Lesson 120 • Writing Synonyms, Antonyms, and Homonyms in Context
Comprehension: Drawing Conclusions

PHONICS ALIVE AT HOME

Ask your child to read the story of his or her name. Together, make up a story for your name.

Name _____

Here's a Hint! In a dictionary, words are listed in **alphabetical order.**

apple   **b**anana   **c**oconut   **d**ate

Write the missing letters to complete the alphabet.
Then **write** each group of words in alphabetical order.

A __ __ D __ __ __ H __ __ K __ __
__ O __ __ R __ __ __ V __ __ Y __

1. riddle	_____	**2.** piano	_____
joke	_____	music	_____
story	_____	violin	_____
tale	_____	trumpet	_____
poem	_____	flute	_____
3. laugh	_____	**4.** you	_____
giggle	_____	me	_____
chuckle	_____	I	_____
smile	_____	we	_____
roar	_____	us	_____

Look at the letter beneath each line. Finish decoding the riddle by **writing** the next letter in the alphabet.

___ ___ ___ A ___ ___ ___ ___ ___ ___ ___ A ___ ___ ___
V   G   X   Q   D   M   S   D   K   D   O   G   M   S   R

___ ___ ___ ___ ? ___ ___ ___ A ___ ___ ___ ___ ___ ___
Q   H   B   G   A   D   B   T   R   D   S   G   X

___ ___ ___ ___ ___ ___ ___ ___ ___ A ___ ___ ___ ___
V   N   Q   J   E   N   Q   O   D   M   T   S   R

Alphabetical Order

Here's a Hint!

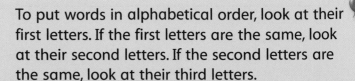

To put words in alphabetical order, look at their first letters. If the first letters are the same, look at their second letters. If the second letters are the same, look at their third letters.

band **b**ed **b**unch   **ba**le **ba**nd **ba**tch

Write each group of words in alphabetical order.

1.

termite _____

turtle _____

toad _____

tadpole _____

tiger _____

2.

slaw _____

stew _____

shrimp _____

soup _____

salad _____

3.

fly _____

flock _____

flew _____

flamingo _____

flutter _____

4.

drum _____

draw _____

drive _____

drop _____

dream _____

Work Together

Put each set of words in alphabetical order to **write** a sentence. End each sentence with a period. Take turns **reading** the sentences with a partner.

5. pizzas made yesterday Mac pepperoni many

_____

6. big jumped wall the Angel's over dog

_____

7. twister the said Maria tongue quickly

_____

PHONICS ALIVE AT HOME Have fun alphabetizing words with your child. Try a grocery list, a book title, or a sentence from a book.

Name _____

Here's a Hint! **Guide words** are found at the top of each dictionary page. They show the first and last words, or entries, on the page.

peacock/piano
> **pea•cock** (pē′kok′) a large bird with green, blue, and gold feathers

Read the guide words. **Cross out** the words that do not belong on the same dictionary page.

1. **peacock/piano**	2. **bloom/bride**	3. **heart/hungry**
panda	book	helpful
phonics	bulldog	high
peacock	better	honor
pelican	bread	hut
peek	blue	hungry
4. **wagon/wind**	5. **light/lucky**	6. **read/roar**
will	loop	ranger
waffle	litter	road
week	lung	rib
wait	low	rule
wish	left	report

Find the path. Go from **Start** to **Finish**. **Connect** the words that would be found on a dictionary page with guide words **change/coin.**

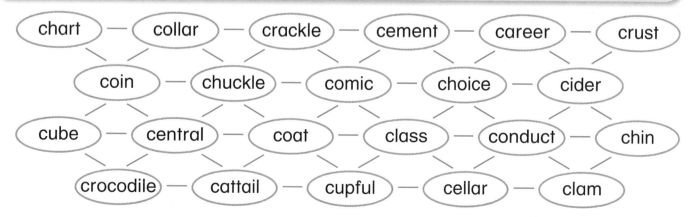

chart — collar — crackle — cement — career — crust

coin — chuckle — comic — choice — cider

cube — central — coat — class — conduct — chin

crocodile — cattail — cupful — cellar — clam

Visit **www.sadlierphonicsonline.com** for another activity with guide words.

Guide Words

Work Together

Where in the dictionary would you find the words in the box? Work with a partner to **write** each word under the correct guide words.

snail	share	swan	school	same	sting
slide	subtract	someday	slow	squeal	sash
stamp	secret	sympathy	sky	seal	speak

1. sack/ship

_____
_____
_____
_____
_____
_____

2. six/spoil

_____
_____
_____
_____
_____
_____

3. square/system

_____
_____
_____
_____
_____
_____

Read each sentence. **Circle** the word that the guide words could help you find in a dictionary.

light/line   **4.** People have always liked listening to stories.

uncle/unit   **5.** Stories help us understand our past.

always/another   **6.** In ancient times Aesop told stories to teach lessons.

table/tease   **7.** Pioneers told tales around the campfire.

Japan/jewel   **8.** Kings hired court jesters to tell stories and jokes.

in/inside   **9.** In western Africa griots had an important job.

heart/houseboat   **10.** They handed down the history of their people.

Write on Track

Alphabetize each group of words you listed at the top of the page.

PHONICS ALIVE AT HOME Review items 4–10 with your child. Ask your child to explain how he or she completed the exercises.

Name _____

Here's a Hint! To quickly find words in a dictionary, turn to the **beginning, middle,** or **end.**

⭐ Where in the dictionary would you find the words in the box? **Write** each word under the correct heading.

laughter	zoo	giggle	noise	humor	knock
delight	jester	yellow	blue	question	wise
funny	silly	television	vitamin	action	octopus

1. Beginning: A–I	**2.** Middle: J–Q	**3.** End: R–Z
_____	_____	_____
_____	_____	_____
_____	_____	_____
_____	_____	_____
_____	_____	_____
_____	_____	_____
_____	_____	_____

⭐ Write **Beginning, Middle,** or **End** to tell where in the dictionary each word in **bold** print can be found.

4. Sometimes Americans speak in an **unusual** way. _____

5. We say that we "catch a **cold**"—or a train! _____

6. **Sometimes** we "lend a hand"—or an ear. _____

7. **Expressions** like these are called idioms. _____

8. "You're **pulling** my leg" means "you're joking." _____

9. During a **rainstorm,** it's "raining cats and dogs." _____

10. Idioms sound strange, but we know what they **mean.** _____

11. Can you think of an **idiom** you have used? _____

Beginning letters are **A–I,** middle letters are **J–Q,** and end letters are **R–Z. Write Beginning, Middle,** or **End** to tell where in the dictionary each word can be found. **Fill in** the circle next to the correct guide words.

1. pride _____

   ○ **press/prince**　　○ **phone/piano**　　○ **prop/prowl**

2. league _____

   ○ **laundry/lay**　　○ **lay/lean**　　○ **leek/lend**

3. bundle _____

   ○ **bullet/bungle**　　○ **burst/byte**　　○ **bud/bulldog**

4. mob _____

   ○ **mistake/moat**　　○ **misty/mob**　　○ **mock/modern**

5. school _____

   ○ **scare/scene**　　○ **school/score**　　○ **scrape/sea**

6. gaggle _____

   ○ **get/giggle**　　○ **garden/gear**　　○ **gab/game**

7. roundup _____

   ○ **river/robot**　　○ **root/roundup**　　○ **row/rubbish**

8. flock _____

   ○ **flesh/flip**　　○ **fly/fog**　　○ **flock/flute**

9. team _____

   ○ **tax/tea**　○ **teen/ten**　　○ **taxi/teddy bear**

10. wave _____

    ○ **water/wax**　　○ **wax/wear**　　○ **weak/weave**

11. nest _____

    ○ **nest/new**　　○ **neck/need**　　○ **net/night**

12. collection _____

    ○ **circle/clutter**　　○ **cobweb/coin**　　○ **cocoon/collection**

PHONICS ALIVE AT HOME

Ask your child to locate five of the words in a dictionary or explain how to locate the words.

Name _____

Here's a Hint! Words called **homographs** have more than one entry in the dictionary. Homographs are spelled the same, but have different meanings.

Read the dictionary entries. **Read** each sentence and **write** the number of the entry that tells the meaning of the word in **bold** print.

> **bark¹** (bärk), the protective covering of a tree
> **bark²** (bärk), the sound made by a dog

1. My dog will **bark** if a stranger comes near. ____

2. The **bark** of a birch tree is white. ____

> **bat¹** (bat), a club used to hit the ball in baseball
> **bat²** (bat), a flying mammal

3. If you get the ball, I'll bring the **bat.** ____

4. The **bat** spread its wings and flew off. ____

> **can¹** (kan), to be able to do something
> **can²** (kan), a metal container for storing something

5. Dad opened a **can** of juice. ____

6. What **can** I do to help you? ____

> **fair¹** (fer), giving the same treatment to everyone
> **fair²** (fer), a showing of farm goods

7. A judge must always be **fair.** ____

8. My pig won first prize at the county **fair.** ____

> **story¹** (stôr′ē), a tale of some events
> **story²** (stôr′ē), the rooms on one level of a building

9. Keisha's room is on the second **story.** ____

10. That was the best **story** I ever read! ____

Read the dictionary entries. **Read** each sentence and **write** the number of the entry that tells the meaning of the word in **bold** print.

---

clip¹ (klip), to cut
clip² (klip), to attach or fasten

---

1. You can use these scissors to **clip** the coupons. ____

2. Please **clip** the papers together. ____

---

fan¹ (fan), a machine that moves air
fan² (fan), a person who strongly admires something

---

3. A true baseball **fan** hates to miss a game. ____

4. If the room gets warm, turn on the **fan**. ____

---

match¹ (mach), a short piece of wood or cardboard used for lighting a fire
match² (mach), to be the same or go together

---

5. Use a **match** to light the candles. ____

6. Look for curtains that **match** the carpet. ____

---

rare¹ (rer), unusual
rare² (rer), not cooked for very long

---

7. Snow is **rare** in this part of the country. ____

8. I cooked the meat longer because it was too **rare**. ____

---

stable¹ (stā′bəl), a building where horses are kept
stable² (stā′bəl), firm or steady

---

9. This old chair is not **stable**. ____

10. Michael led the pony back to the **stable**. ____

Write on Track

Look up the word **shed** in the dictionary. How many entries do you find? Write a sentence for each entry.

PHONICS ALIVE AT HOME Choose a pair of homographs. Together, write a new sentence for each word in the pair.

Here's a Hint! If a word has more than one meaning, it will have more than one dictionary definition.

Read the dictionary entry. Read each sentence and **write** the number of the definition that tells the meaning of the word in **bold** print.

> **foot** (fút), **I** the end of a leg   **2** the lowest part

1. Julia kicked the ball with her **foot.** ____

2. Jake left his backpack near the **foot** of the stairs. ____

> **head** (hed), **I** the upper part of the body where the eyes, ears, nose, mouth, and brain are   **2** the striking or cutting part of a tool

3. I wear a hat on my **head** when I go out in the sun. ____

4. I hit my thumb with the **head** of the hammer. ____

> **plot** (plot), **I** the events in a story   **2** a small piece of ground

5. I set aside a **plot** for a vegetable garden. ____

6. The **plot** was so exciting that I couldn't put down the book. ____

> **trunk** (trungk), **I** the main stem of a tree   **2** a large box with a lid

7. The **trunk** of that sequoia tree is very wide. ____

8. Let me help you pack your **trunk.** ____

> **wing** (wing), **I** the part of an animal's body used for flying   **2** a part that sticks out from the main part of a building

9. The park ranger helped a bird with an injured **wing.** ____

10. The gym is in the new **wing** of the school. ____

Read the dictionary entry. **Read** each sentence and **write** the number of the definition that tells the meaning of the word in **bold** print.

> **beam** (bēm), **I** a long, large piece of wood or metal   **2** a ray of light

1. The **beam** of the flashlight lit the way. ____

2. The carpenter nailed the **beam** in place. ____

> **cast** (kast), **I** the actors in a show   **2** a stiff dressing or mold used to hold a broken bone in place

3. When the play was over, the **cast** came out on stage. ____

4. The doctor put a **cast** on Ariel's broken arm. ____

> **check** (chek), **I** a mark made to show that something is correct or has been noted   **2** a slip of paper showing how much is owed for a restaurant meal

5. The waiter brought the **check** to the table. ____

6. The teacher put a **check** next to each correct answer. ____

> **deck** (dek), **I** the floor of a ship   **2** a pack of playing cards

7. Captain Jack ordered the sailors to wash the **deck.** ____

8. Robert picked eight cards from the **deck.** ____

> **model** (mod′əl), **I** a small copy of something   **2** a person whose job it is to wear clothing or makeup that is for sale

9. The **model** wore a blue suit. ____

10. Adam built a **model** of an airplane. ____

> **screen** (skrēn), **I** the surface on which a movie is projected **2** wire netting

11. The **screen** on the window keeps flies out. ____

12. This theater has a wide **screen.** ____

PHONICS ALIVE AT HOME   Choose one of the dictionary entries. Together, write a new sentence for each definition.

Name _____

 Write each group of words in alphabetical order.

1.

run   _____

touchdown   _____

goal   _____

basket   _____

point   _____

2.

orange   _____

grape   _____

lime   _____

lemon   _____

cherry   _____

3.

monkey   _____

leopard   _____

zebra   _____

lion   _____

giraffe   _____

4.

Trent   _____

Thomas   _____

Truman   _____

Tammy   _____

Tucker   _____

 Read the guide words. **Circle** the words that belong on the same dictionary page.

5. **idea/inch**

ignore
impossible
ice
imagine
index

6. **zero/zoo**

zone
zoom
zipper
zebra
zigzag

7. **panda/pass**

parade
pancake
patch
paper
partner

8. **fix/fold**

fish
flag
flea
focus
fox

9. **near/next**

neigh
nice
navy
news
need

10. **dancer/decide**

dare
deal
daylight
damp
deed

 Help explain each riddle by **writing** two definitions for each word in **bold** print.

What can you use to mend a broken watermelon?
A watermelon **patch!**

1. _____

2. _____

I have **eyes,** but I can't see. What am I?
A potato.

3. _____

4. _____

I have three **feet,** but no toes. What am I?
A yardstick.

5. _____

6. _____

Why is a baseball game like a pancake?
They both need the **batter.**

7. _____

8. _____

What do you **serve,** but never eat?
A tennis ball!

9. _____

10. _____

 PHONICS ALIVE AT HOME Together, make up riddles based on these words with more than one meaning: **bark, trunk, wing, head.**

Name _____

Let's **read** and **talk** about the different uses of some English words.

Learn About Words Used in England

Imagine your family is going to drive through England this summer. The following tips from an English auto club may help you plan ahead.

1. Pack the **boot** of the **auto** carefully.

2. Keep a litterbag in the front for potato **crisp** bags and other snack wrappers.

3. Before your trip, stop at a **petrol** station. Ask the worker to lift the **bonnet** and check the oil.

4. If a big **lorry** suddenly **overtakes** you, don't cut off the driver. You don't want to get a dent in the **wing.**

What synonyms would you use for the words in **bold** print?

Do you know of other terms or phrases that are used differently in another country or in another section of the United States?

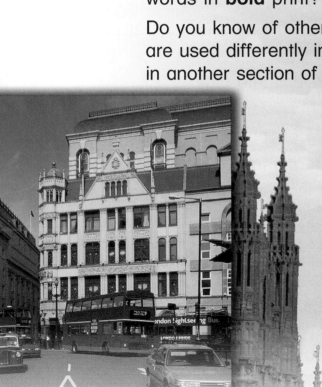

Lesson 127 • Synonyms, Antonyms, Homonyms, and Dictionary Skills in Context
Comprehension: Comparing and Contrasting
Developing Fluency

219

 Check-Up **Read** the guide words. **Cross out** the word that does not belong on the same dictionary page. **Write** the remaining words in alphabetical order.

1. **vary/violin**

vase

violet _____

vest _____

vine _____

valentine _____

2. **leave/lump**

litterbug

lucky _____

lunch _____

lime _____

leave _____

3. **eight/empty**

elbow

empty _____

eel _____

eight _____

election _____

4. **waltz/wise**

within

weekend _____

whistle _____

water _____

web _____

Check-Up **Read** each sentence. **Fill in** the circle next to the correct meaning of the word in **bold** print.

5. What will you **serve** at your party?
   ◯ offer to others   ◯ put a ball into play

6. The **story** you told made me laugh.
   ◯ tale about events   ◯ level of a building

7. Can you thread the needle, or is the **eye** too small?
   ◯ body part by which you see   ◯ hole in a needle

8. What's the **plot** of the book?
   ◯ main story   ◯ piece of ground

9. Lucky's **bark** is loud, but he doesn't bite.
   ◯ tree covering   ◯ sound a dog makes

10. Let me show you around the school's new **wing.**
   ◯ animal part used for flying   ◯ part of the building

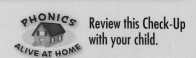 **PHONICS ALIVE AT HOME** Review this Check-Up with your child.

Reading at Home: Share the book with family and friends. Why do you think someone would write a joke book?

Name _____

A Laugh A Day!

What's your favorite kind of joke? Do you like to hear or tell knock-knocks, riddles or puns? Do jokes help you to think about words in a new way? See which kind of joke in this book seems the funniest to you. Remember: It's important to laugh at least once a day!

— Fold —

Puns

It's raining cats and dogs outside! I know. I just stepped in a poodle.

I saw a catfish yesterday. Really? How did it hold the pole?

Write the funniest joke you know. Remember to share it with someone who needs a laugh.

_____
_____
_____
_____
_____

 DIRECTIONS: Cut and fold the book.

Lesson 128 • Units 5–7 Take-Home Book
Comprehension: Determining
Author's Purpose

221

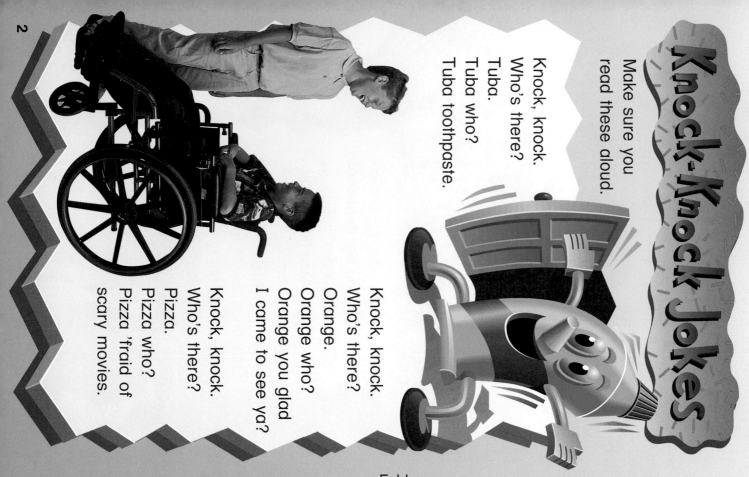

2

Knock-Knock Jokes

Make sure you read these aloud.

Knock, knock.
Who's there?
Tuba.
Tuba who?
Tuba toothpaste.

Knock, knock.
Who's there?
Orange.
Orange who?
Orange you glad
I came to see ya?

Knock, knock.
Who's there?
Pizza.
Pizza who?
Pizza 'fraid of
scary movies.

Fold

Riddles

Ha! Ha! Ha!

Why do birds fly south for
the winter?
They can't afford to take the train.

What kind of deer carry umbrellas?
Reindeer!

What coat is usable only when it's wet?
A coat of paint!

Where do fish keep their life savings?
In a river bank!

BANK

3

Name _____ Year 20____ –20____

My Progress Checklist

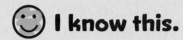 **I need to practice this.** ☺ **I know this.**

Unit 1: Consonants and Consonant Variants

○ ☺ Consonants at the beginning of words
○ ☺ Consonants at the end of words
○ ☺ Consonants in the middle of words
○ ☺ Soft and hard **c**
○ ☺ Soft and hard **g**
○ ☺ Sounds of **s**

Unit 2: Short and Long Vowels

○ ☺ Short vowel **a**   ○ ☺ Long vowel **a**
○ ☺ Short vowel **i**   ○ ☺ Long vowel **i**
○ ☺ Short vowel **o**   ○ ☺ Long vowel **o**
○ ☺ Short vowel **u**   ○ ☺ Long vowel **u**
○ ☺ Short vowel **e**   ○ ☺ Long vowel **e**

Unit 3: Syllables, Consonant Blends, Compound Words, y as a Vowel, Silent Letters, and Consonant Digraphs

○ ☺ Recognize syllables   ○ ☺ Silent letters in **gn, mb**
○ ☺ **l** blends   ○ ☺ **th**
○ ☺ **r** blends   ○ ☺ **sh**
○ ☺ **s** blends   ○ ☺ **wh**
○ ☺ **tw**   ○ ☺ **ch**
○ ☺ Blends at the end of words   ○ ☺ **ck**
○ ☺ Compound words   ○ ☺ **ph**
○ ☺ Words with **y** at the end ○ ☺ **gh**
○ ☺ Silent letters in **kn, wr**

Unit 4: r-Controlled Vowels, Vowel Digraphs, and Diphthongs

○ 🙂 **ar** and **or**	○ 🙂 **ei**	○ 🙂 **al**
○ 🙂 **er, ir, ur, ear**	○ 🙂 **oo**	○ 🙂 **ow** and **ou**
○ 🙂 **air, are, eer**	○ 🙂 **au**	○ 🙂 **oi, oy, ew**
○ 🙂 **ea**	○ 🙂 **aw**	

Unit 5: Syllables, Contractions, and Word Endings

○ 🙂 VCCV and VCCCV words	○ 🙂 Singular possessives
○ 🙂 VCV words	○ 🙂 Plural possessives
○ 🙂 Words ending in **le**	○ 🙂 Inflectional ending **s**
○ 🙂 Schwa	○ 🙂 Inflectional ending **es**
○ 🙂 Contractions	○ 🙂 Inflectional ending **ing**
○ 🙂 Plurals with **s**	○ 🙂 Inflectional ending **ed**
○ 🙂 Plurals with **es**	○ 🙂 Spelling changes in
○ 🙂 Plurals for words that	words with inflectional
end in **y**	endings
○ 🙂 Plurals for words that	
end in **f** and **fe**	

Unit 6: Suffixes, Prefixes, and Multisyllabic Words

○ 🙂 **ful, less, ness**	○ 🙂 **en, able, ible**	○ 🙂 **re, un, dis**
○ 🙂 **ly** and **y**	○ 🙂 **ment** and **ion**	○ 🙂 **in** and **im**
○ 🙂 **er** and **est**	○ 🙂 **er, or, ist**	○ 🙂 **pre, de, mis**

Unit 7: Synonyms, Antonyms, Homonyms, and Dictionary Skills

○ 🙂 Synonyms	○ 🙂 Guide words
○ 🙂 Antonyms	○ 🙂 Finding words
○ 🙂 Homonyms	○ 🙂 Homographs
○ 🙂 Alphabetical order	○ 🙂 Multiple-meaning words